P101 - 4 Bs used AS DOMINANTS

TWENTIETH-CENTURY HARMONY

TWENTIETH-CENTURY

HARMONY

Creative Aspects and Practice

BY VINCENT PERSICHETTI

W·W·NORTON & COMPANY · INC · New York

Library of Congress Catalog Card No. 61-5615

PRINTED IN THE UNITED STATES OF AMERICA

2 3 4 5 6 7 8 9

Contents

7 Diff 7th Chords
(p 75)

Page 78 - Omitting parts of 9th chords for
Richness density - solidity - Tension -

77 - 9th chords from Darkest to Brightest

P.88 12-Note CHORDS ARE USED FOR PUNCTUATION

Foreword

THE MUSIC of the first half of the twentieth century has produced a harmonic practice that can be defined. During these sixty years, harmonic ideas have been in constant flux; composers have created new musical devices and techniques. This broad palette of materials has fundamental significance for the present scene, for amalgamation of the various sound formations and techniques is in process. Composers have worked instinctively, with the ear as their guide, and have arrived at something of a common usage of these materials. Contemporary musical resources include a wide range of materials of the past and present, and the available techniques yield abundant expressive returns.

Works of high caliber are plentiful in the twentieth century. The rich mixture of materials and styles is made up of many ingredients: rhythmic energy, vivid harmonic fabric, melodic color, and fresh linear writing. There are bold statements and delicate embellishments, moments of fancy, and developmental forces that refuse to be bound by a severe formal plan. There are daringly experimental and strongly traditional forces which bring divergent materials together.

The various harmonic devices do not, in themselves, account for creative writing. Only when theory and technique are combined with imagination and talent do works of importance result. Nevertheless, a practical knowledge of twentieth-century harmonic resources is a requirement for both performer and composer. The performer is offered specific information, and the composer, workable materials.

Twentieth-Century Harmony is not a speculative treatise nor one proposing a personal mode of organization. Rather, it is an account of specific harmonic materials commonly used by twentieth-century composers. Although knowledge of materials and technique does not in itself create a personal style, precision in the choice of notes and understanding of harmonic devices are desirable in perfecting a means of expression and in stating a musical idea clearly and consistently.

This text aims to define this harmonic activity and make it available to the student and young composer. A detailed study of the essential harmonic technique of the twentieth century is presented, according to the practice of contemporary composers. The book is for and about creativity; it presents musical possibilities to stimulate creative musical thought. Specific media are called for, but substitutions may and should be made depending upon the instrumentalists and vocalists available in the classroom or to the composer. Most exercises require originally conceived melody and harmony in a rhythmic frame; tempo, dynamics, and phrasing are fundamental considerations. The applications do not in themselves supply adequate training, but are offered as suggestions for the invention of further examples. Passages from the literature are not reproduced out of context; exact page locations are listed under the heading "Source Material." None of the examples represent rare cases or exceptional musical coincidences; they do offer representative twentieth-century harmonic methods.

This text may be used in advanced harmony courses and as a point of departure in literature of music courses in colleges and conservatories; or it may form the harmonic basis of a first-year composition course for both composition and noncomposition majors. The division of musical study into separate segments—melody, counterpoint, harmony, rhythm, and form—is advisable

only if the interdependence of these forces as found in the literature is maintained. Reference is made to contrapuntal, formal, and
orchestral devices, for harmonic and contrapuntal movement are
affected by a work's form and medium. The way various chordal
structures are built, the reasons they sound as they do, the connection of the chords and their suitability for differing conditions,
consistency of texture, and the combining of contrasting textures
must be understood.

Following a predetermined path of strict axioms is avoided, for
harmonic creativity depends upon the relation of chord to chord
in a particular context; any chord may progress to any other chord,
and seemingly opposing techniques may be combined under certain formal and dramatic conditions. In theoretical deductions the
emphasis is placed upon creative ideas and compositional stimula-
tion.

Composers have, in their music, coordinated the various musical
resources of the early part of the century. Significant creators
working actively in many media have given impetus to a flourish-
ing twentieth-century music, have given it pulse and creative
health. The embryonic composer has a technical heritage. Little
can stand in his way if he possesses creative talent.

| # Intervals

Any tone can succeed any other tone, any tone can sound simultaneously with any other tone or tones, and any group of tones can be followed by any other group of tones, just as any degree of tension or nuance can occur in any medium under any kind of stress or duration. Successful projection will depend upon the contextual and formal conditions that prevail, and upon the skill and the soul of the composer.

An understanding of the harmonic process may begin with an understanding of the melodic and harmonic intervals of sound.

CONSTRUCTION

An interval, like any other musical sound, may have different meanings for different composers. While its physical properties are constant, its usage changes with the working context to which it belongs.

For centuries theorists have, through the science of acoustics, observed degrees of interval tension and from this has been evolved a concept of the relative consonant-dissonant qualities of intervals. Although this consonant-dissonant concept is affected by countless factors within any given style, and may vary considerably from one age to another, the notes of an isolated interval—whether sounded simultaneously or successively—do have a basic quality. This quality is determined by the interval's own particular physical properties of sound waves and overtones.

An isolated tone, when sounded, generates a series of overtones which form intervals that relate to each other by mathematical ratio. Generally, in the tempered scale, consonant intervals are considered to be those formed from the lower tones of the overtone series (see Ex. 1-21), the upper overtones producing dissonant intervals. In practice, these tone-to-tone relationships have been reduced by the use of the chromatic tempered scale from an unlimited number of intervals to twelve intervals which retain the characteristics of their counterparts in the overtone series. Their textural characteristics are as follows:

perfect fifth and octave—open consonances
major and minor thirds and sixths—soft consonances
minor seconds and major sevenths—sharp dissonances
major seconds and minor sevenths—mild dissonances
perfect fourth—consonant or dissonant
tritone (augmented fourth or diminished fifth)—ambiguous, can
be either neutral or restless

Ex. 1-1

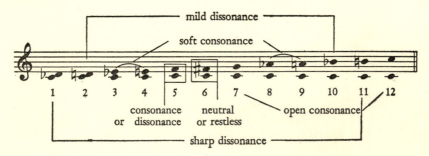

It is difficult to classify the tritone and the perfect fourth out of musical context. The tritone divides the octave at its halfway point and is the least stable of the intervals. It sounds primarily neutral in chromatic passages and restless in diatonic passages.

Ex. 1-2

The perfect fourth sounds consonant in dissonant surroundings and dissonant in consonant surroundings.

Ex. 1-3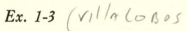

Intervals can follow each other in any order and may be arranged to form any pattern of tension interplay. For example, a series of intervals may begin with an interval of little tension and end with an interval of great tension. The quality of the perfect fourth and tritone will be determined solely by context.

Ex. 1-4

This is how such a tension arrangement might sound in practice.

Ex. 1-5

Next the tension pattern is reversed; intervals of great tension move to those of relative repose. The ambiguous tritone at the end now assumes a neutral character.

Ex. 1-6

Intervallic tension may be used to suit any design or function of the music. The consonant-dissonant properties of intervals may be used to support or oppose, for various expressive purposes, other forces such as instrumental timbre, dynamics, and tempo. Sharp dissonances seem consistent in double reeds playing loudly. However, the same intervals assigned the timbre of muted strings create an entirely different effect. The feeling of one is raucous and of the other, introspective—one gives the impression of intervallic tension disagreement with other compositional forces, and the other the impression of agreement.

Ex. 1-7

As composers' attitudes and practices change, the concept of consonance and dissonance may change. Various degrees of tension may be accepted as consonance. Consonant intervals may sound dissonant in a passage dominated by dissonant intervals, and in harmony comprised of strongly dissonant intervals these dissonances often become the "consonant" norm of the musical organization.

INVERSION AND SPACING

When intervals are inverted, their consonant-dissonant quality changes because the spacing and register have been altered. The extent of change varies with the individual interval. Inverting the perfect fifth alters its basic function, this solid interval becoming an unstable perfect fourth. When sharp dissonances are inverted, marked changes in intensity occur. The cutting minor second opens into a widespreading major seventh and thereby loses some of its sting. Inverting the tritone causes a pronounced shift in register even though no change in intervallic distance has taken place.

If intervals are spaced more than an octave apart, the soft consonances (thirds and sixths) become richer; open consonances (octaves and fifths) and the consonant perfect fourth become stronger:

Ex. 1-8   (♩ = 60)

Dissonances (seconds and sevenths) become less biting, yet more brilliant.

Ex. 1-9

The tritone, neutral in chromatic progressions, becomes more ambiguous and veiled; restless in diatonic progressions, it becomes even less addicted to resolution.

Ex. 1-10

INTERVALS IN CHORDS

Two or more intervals occurring simultaneously form what is usually felt to be a chord. Chords may be built with equidistant intervals,

Ex. 1-11

with different kinds (major, minor, etc.) of the same interval number,

Ex. 1-12

and with mixed intervals.

Ex. 1-13

Before a chord is set in harmonic motion the consonant-dissonant quality of each interval contained in the chord should be noted. It is only by making use of differences in chordal values as determined by interval characteristics that harmonic tension can be controlled. Without this kind of freedom only a limited kind of harmonic progression can be achieved, that which results from root relationships within a fixed scale and key. Awareness of intervallic tension produces harmonic movement of a more flexible nature. Good part-writing is, of course, necessary to achieve such flexibility.

A three-note chord has three intervals; observe the possible variants in consonant-dissonant combinations.

Ex. 1-14

3 cons.   2 cons. &   1 cons. &   2 cons. &   1 cons., 1 mild   1 mild &
          1 mild diss. 2 mild, diss. 1 sharp diss. & 1 sharp diss. 2 sharp diss.

A four-note chord contains six intervallic factors, and a five-note chord, ten.

Ex. 1-15

3 cons., 2 sharp, 1 neut. diss.   7 cons., 2 mild, 1 sharp diss.

The quality of chordal tension affects and is affected by dynamics, medium, and spacing, but varies in different musical contexts. Handling these harmonic materials becomes simpler if some general classification of the intervallic characteristics of chords is applied. All chords fall generally into one of two categories, those chords that contain at least one sharp dissonance and those that contain no sharp dissonance. Each category may be subdivided into those chords containing at least one tritone and those containing no tritone.

Ex. 1-16

Chords containing a tritone tend to have a restless quality, while those without tritones have stability even when extremely dissonant.

The presence of a perfect fourth in a chord lends ambiguity because of this interval's ability to function either as consonance or dissonance; other intervals in the chord must determine its character, the chord being classifiable only in its total interval context. The consonant-dissonant quality of chords containing a perfect fourth is defined by the interval formed by the bass note and the note not involved with the fourth. When this interval is a mild or sharp dissonance, the perfect fourth sounds like an open consonance; when it is a soft consonance the perfect fourth sounds mildly dissonant.

Ex. 1-17

Any kind of chord has, under "normal" conditions, its own natural doubling, such as the doubling of roots in major triads. It is possible, however, to write a chord in numerous other ways. Actually, any note may be doubled, tripled, or omitted for specific textural purposes. Doubling may be used to enrich simple chords, to point up characteristic part-writing, or to strengthen certain parts of a chord. A doubled major third adds color and a doubled dissonant tone increases the bite. Excessive coupling (all voices doubled) produces percussive-sounding harmony.

Chord members may be so arranged that specific kinds of intervals monopolize the musical pattern.

Ex. 1-18

The chosen interval may form separate intervallic strands that move in contrary motion.

Ex. 1-19

Spacing is an inseparable part of the character of a tonal structure. For ordinary balance, the wide intervals are placed at the bottom of the chord; for tautness, the wide intervals are placed at the top. For evenly distributed tension, all instruments or voices are employed in their grateful registers and altered accordingly if specific harmonic stresses or highlights are desired.

Closely spaced harmony crowded with small intervals clears when each chord is broken into a succession of intervals in two-part writing.

Ex. 1-20

But harmony that is clouded may remain so and be effective; both cloudy and clear chordal materials are essential ingredients in musical composition. The overtone series is useful in measuring the aural difference.

OVERTONE INFLUENCE

Any tone generates a series of overtones or partials that reach upward indefinitely, though not all are audible.

Ex. 1-21

A tone has both vertical and horizontal implications; its overtones may be used simultaneously in chordal structures or consecutively in melodic lines. Some sounding bodies produce higher overtones than others. A tone produced on an instrument capable of generating high overtones recognizable by the ear can have a quality that is resonant and relatively dissonant because of the crowding of the upper partials. The same note played on a medium having overtones that stop aurally with the lower or middle partials will sound relatively consonant, but lack resonance. Such are some of the differences that help give instruments their individual tone quality.

Basic harmonic materials may be traced to the overtone series, but only general facts concerning chordal structure and resonance are indicated by the partials. A triad is formed by partials 1-3-5 (root, fifth, and third), a seventh chord by 1-3-5-7, a ninth chord by 1-3-5-7-9, the whole-tone chords by 7 to 11, chords by fourths by 6-8-9, and the augmented fourth chord by 6-8-11. However, deduction concerning harmonic implications of partials beyond the 6th is not wholly practicable because the tempered scale does not coincide in pitch with the 7th, 11th, 13th, and 14th partials. It is quite possible to relate multi-note chords by thirds to the series but the overtones produce limited resonance. The major triad (partials 1-3-5) is clearly in tune. But the seventh partial is slightly less than a minor third from the sixth, and if considered as the seventh (in chords by thirds) misinterprets the natural phenomenon. Our tempered aural thinking can include tones up to the sixth partial but beyond that point the aural perception is merely rational. The acoustician's observations are useful to the composer only if blended with artistic intuition.

The fifth (partial 3) is a lower partial than the third (partial 5) and consequently is more powerful; this is an important factor in understanding relationships of tones, chords, and tonalities. Resonant harmony is not formed by seeking higher and higher overtones but by using overtones of overtones. For example, in a C-E-G-B chord, the seventh (B) is the fifth above the third (E). In this sense both C and E are accompanied by their fifths and therefore have strong relationships with these other tones. If we wish to add an additional resonant tone, we should add not a higher, weaker overtone of C (such as F♯) but a lower and stronger overtone of an overtone (such as G♯ which is partial No. 5 of E).

Ex. 1-22

Chordal structures are most resonant when the distances between the members are somewhat similar to those in the overtone series (wide spacing in the lower register and close spacing in the upper register). The overtone series sets a norm for brilliance. For maximum brilliance, let the lower tones of the chord be accompanied by their own overtones.

The resonant properties of an instrument or of objects surrounding the performer create additional sonority that underpins the sound. The principle of supporting resonance by lower sonority is occasionally applied to chordal structures. This color device is used primarily when the composer works with chords in the upper register and needs to fill in toward the bass. In lower registers, the addition of tones is limited by the danger of muddy progressions. Most effective supporting tones are the fifth or ninth below the bottom tone of the chord because the fifth is a strong and resonant interval and the ninth is a fifth below the fifth. Basses plucking the fifth or ninth below the actual bass line cast a reflected sheen over the harmony.

Ex. 1-23

MEDIUM

The medium to which a musical idea is given has a direct bearing upon harmonic writing, as do intervallic texture, spacing, and dynamics. The following passages are built upon the same chordal

progression but are conceived in completely different media
and this results in completely different kinds of harmonic settings.
Chordal tension, spacing, and dynamics have changed drastically
in each version.

Ex. 1-24

Awareness of timbre is essential to good harmonic craft. Quality
of tone as defined by medium plays a functional role in harmonic
movement. Music written for the piano is effective on the piano,
but that written for orchestra gives an improper impression when
played on the piano. Harmonic writing should be conceived for
the medium employed.

For example, orchestral color may soften the extreme dissonance
of thirteenth chords, rob the triad of its soft consonance, or alter
chordal direction. The high register of keyboard instruments or
the harmonics of strings add brilliance to parallel harmony. Clusters
binding seconds may be loosened by the selection of certain tones

to sound as thirds in separate orchestral choirs. Polychords are made transparent when each triad or unit within the composite structure is sounded by a separate orchestral section. Pizzicato strings define uncertain passing tones in woodwind voices, and a harp may underline obscure rhythms in lagging strings.

Source Material

(red.) = a reduced score (piano, two pianos, or piano-vocal)

Two-part writing in a two-voice work:

Béla Bartók, 44 Violin Duets (Boosey)
Arthur Berger, Duo for Oboe and Clarinet (Peters)
Pierre Boulez, Le Marteau Sans Maître, Mvt. III (Universal)
Alberto Ginastera, Duo for Flute and Oboe (Mercury)
Paul Hindemith, Zwei Kanonische Duette (Schott)
Arthur Honegger, Sonatine for Two Violins (Sirène)
Bohuslav Martinu, Three Madrigals for Violin and Viola (Boosey)
Walter Piston, Duo for Viola and Cello (Associated)
Francis Poulenc, Sonata for Two Clarinets (Chester)
Serge Prokofiev, Sonata for Two Violins (Russe)
Maurice Ravel, Sonate pour Violon et Violoncelle (Durand)
Heitor Villa-Lobos, Choros No. 2 for Flute and Clarinet (Eschig) *p 15*

Two-part writing in a work of more than two voices:

Henk Badings, String Quartet No. 2, p. 9 (Schott)
Bruno Bettinelli, Sinfonia Breve, p. 1 (Ricordi)
Aaron Copland, Piano Sonata, pp. 23–24 (Boosey)
Hans Werner Henze, Drei Dithyramben (orchestra), p. 44 (Schott)
Paul Hindemith, Organ Sonata No. 1, p. 17 (Schott)
Vagn Holmboe, Kammerkoncert No. 2, p. 24 (Dania)
Benjamin Lees, Fantasia for Piano, p. 4 (Boosey)
Peter Mennin, Five Piano Pieces, pp. 2–5 (C. Fischer)
Walter Piston, Sonata for Violin and Piano, p. 20 (Arrow)
William Schuman, Symphony No. 4, p. 1 (G. Schirmer)
Dmitri Shostakovich, Piano Quintet, p. 39 (Am-Rus)
Igor Stravinsky, Threni (red.), pp. 5, 9, 15, 48 (Boosey)
Kurt Weill, Mahagonny (red.), p. 3 (Universal)

Two-part coupled writing:

Béla Bartók, Mikrokosmos, Vol. IV, p. 22 (Boosey)
Dmitri Kabalevsky, Piano Sonata No. 2, p. 1 (Leeds)
Ernst Krenek, Jonny Spielt Auf, p. 4 (Universal)
Robert Palmer, Piano Quartet, pp. 19–21 (G. Schirmer for S.P.A.M.)
Goffredo Petrassi, Salmo IX (red.), p. 1 (Ricordi)
Hilding Rosenberg, Piano Sonata No. 3, p. 6 (Nordiska)
Igor Stravinsky, Le Rossignol (red.), p. 3 (Russe)

Passages featuring specific intervals:

Béla Bartók, Concerto for Orchestra, pp. 29–35 (Boosey)
Alban Berg, Fünf Orchester-Lieder, Op. 4 (red.), p. 2 (Universal)
Niels Viggo Bentzon, Third Piano Sonata, p. 29 (Hansen)
Marc Blitzstein, Regina (red.), p. 71 (Chappell)
Benjamin Britten, Billy Budd (red.), p. 7 (Boosey)
Paul Hindemith, Madrigale, p. 65 (Schott)
Arthur Honegger, Judith (red.), p. 110 (Salabert)
Maurice Ravel, L'Heure Espagnole (red.), p. 39 (Durand)
Arnold Schoenberg, Six Little Pieces, Op. 19, II (Universal)
William Schuman, Voyage (for piano), p. 7 (G. Schirmer)
Roger Sessions, Suite from "The Black Maskers," p. 10 (Marks)
Dmitri Shostakovich, Symphony No. 10, pp. 66–67 (Leeds)
Alexandre Tcherepnine, Bagatelles for Piano, p. 2 (Heugel)
Randall Thompson, Alleluia, p. 11 (E. C. Schirmer)

Characteristic spacing:

Aaron Copland, Sonata for Violin and Piano, p. 33 (Boosey)
Wolfgang Fortner, Impromptus for Orchestra, p. 5 (Schott)
Alexei Haieff, Piano Concerto (red.), p. 43 (Boosey)
Karl Amadeus Hartmann, Symphony No. 4, for Strings, p. 38 (Schott)
Paul Hindemith, Symphonie Mathis der Maler, p. 1 (Schott)
Igor Stravinsky, Symphony of Psalms, p. 63 (Boosey)
Guido Turchi, Piccolo Concerto Notturno (orchestra), p. 20 (Ricordi)

Examples of overtones:

William Bergsma, Six Songs, p. 6 (C. Fischer)
Elliott Carter, Piano Sonata, p. 27 (Music Press)
Aaron Copland, Piano Variations, p. 3 (Boosey)
David Diamond, Rounds for String Orchestra, p. 20 (Elkan-Vogel)
Hans Werner Henze, Sonata per Archi, p. 27 (Schott)
Gustav Holst, The Planets, p. 113 (Boosey)
Jean-Louis Martinet, Orphée, p. 19 (Heugel)
Olivier Messiaen, Turangalîla-Symphonie, p. 6 (Durand)

Arnold Schoenberg, Piano Pieces, Op. 11, p. 3 (Universal)
William Schuman, Undertow, p. 40 (G. Schirmer)
Roger Sessions, Piano Sonata No. 2, p. 16 (Marks)
Igor Stravinsky, Sérénade en La, p. 9 (Russe)
Bernd Alois Zimmermann, Konfigurationen, p. 4 (Schott)

Applications

A two- or three-line piano reduction may be used in written examples.

1. Write a phrase for two flutes that contains several dissonant perfect fourths. Follow this phrase with one that contains several consonant perfect fourths.

2. Write a fast and tempestuous passage for two oboes employing no sharp dissonant intervals.

3. Write a soft, lyric passage consisting mostly of dissonant intervals. Score for two muted violins.

4. Extend the following oboe and English horn opening:

Ex. 1-25

5. Write for violin and cello a prelude that contains both a crescendo and diminuendo of interval tension. Do not allow the dynamic level to coincide with the intervallic tension level.

6. Add a second trumpet part to the following trumpet line, employing a crescendo of interval tension:

Ex. 1-26

7. Construct a declamatory phrase for three horns using chords built by equidistant intervals.

8. Write a passage for three clarinets using only chords with one consonant, one mild dissonant, and one sharp dissonant interval. Employ a variety of spacings.

9. Write a passage for string quartet using only chords of mixed intervals.

10. Write a percussive passage for string orchestra using excessive doubling and coupling.

11. Write a scherzando passage for piano using similar intervals in both hands, moving in contrary motion.

12. Move three bassoons quickly through widely spaced consonant chords.

| CHAPTER TWO | Scale Materials |

MODES

A CENTRAL TONE to which other tones are related can establish tonality, and the manner in which these other tones are placed around the central tone produces modality. A great number of scale patterns have been used by twentieth-century composers, but seven stand apart from the others because of their whole-half-step order. Each has its special character, and any tone may be used as the tonic starting point.

Ex. 2-1

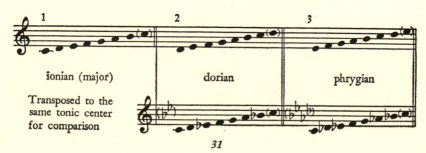

31

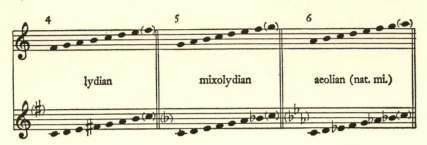

Most of these twentieth-century modes bear the names given them during the Middle Ages but the resemblance is one of construction, not usage. Ionian is the familiar major scale and aeolian, the natural minor; locrian (infrequently used) is unmistakable because of its diminished tonic triad. Of the four remaining modes, two have major tonic and two have minor tonic triads. Lydian consists of the major scale with the fourth scale step raised; mixolydian of the major scale with the leading tone lowered. Dorian is the natural minor with its sixth step raised; and phrygian, the natural minor with the second scale step lowered.

The distinctive flavor of these last four modes is exploited by employing harmonic progressions in which the characteristic scale step occurs often. This tone keeps the mode from becoming a major or natural minor scale. For example, a lydian passage on D should contain a high percentage of chords that include the tone G♯ (raised fourth step); otherwise the lydian flavor will be lost.

A set of chords may be found within the diatonic limits of each mode. As in major and minor modes, there is a definite relation between primary and secondary chordal materials. The primary chords are the tonic, plus two dominant equivalents. These double dominants are those major or minor triads that include the characteristic scale step which produces the principal flavor of the mode. In each mode there lurks a diminished triad; this is a difficult chord because its diminished fifth tends to suggest the dominant seventh of the major key with the same number of sharps or flats as the mode in question.

In the lydian mode with its characteristic fourth step (major scale with the raised fourth), the primary chords are I, II, and VII and the secondary are III, V, and VI. The diminished triad is IV. With the lydian on D, for example, this works out as follows.

D lydian (characteristic flavor: 4th step):

Ex. 2-2

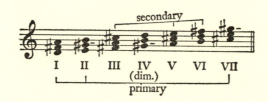

In the mixolydian mode with its characteristic seventh step (major scale with the lowered seventh) the primary chords are I, V, and VII and the secondary chords are II, IV, and VI. The diminished triad is III.

D mixolydian (characteristic flavor: 7th step):

Ex. 2-3

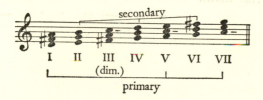

In the dorian mode, with its characteristic sixth step (natural minor scale with the raised sixth), the primary chords are I, II, and IV and the secondary chords are III, V, and VII. The diminished triad is VI.

D dorian (characteristic flavor: 6th step):

Ex. 2-4

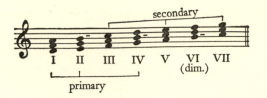

In the phrygian mode with its characteristic second step (natural minor with the lowered second) the primary chords are I, II, and VII and the secondary are III, IV, and VI. The diminished triad is V.

D phrygian (characteristic flavor: 2nd step):

Ex. 2-5

Modal chords by thirds, other than triads, need special attention because the tritone present in many seventh and ninth chords implies the dominant seventh of a major scale; the chord may then easily lose its tonic feeling and slip into a major scale. Useful seventh and ninth chords in the modes (excepting ionian) are those involving no tritone.

Phrygian seventh chords:

Ex. 2-6

Phrygian ninth chords:

Ex. 2-7

Triads, sevenths, and ninths progress easily from one to another while in the same mode:

Ex. 2-8

Chord succession of any kind is not just a series of separate root points but a harmonic relationship in which chords move forward. The selection and distribution of primary and secondary chords within a given segment of music and the ways in which the harmonic rhythm is organized help give the music its individual sound.

A single mode is not necessarily used throughout an entire section. As working materials for composition the modes may be arranged effectively according to their tension relationships. The greatest number of flats that can be applied to a modal scale on a particular tone will produce the "darkest" mode, the locrian. Subtracting flats (and then adding sharps) in diatonic signature order will produce an arrangement of modes from "darkest" to "brightest." The dorian mode is the middle point and sets the norm.

Ex. 2-9

mixolydian   ionian   lydian

Within this related order a flexible set of modes is at the composer's disposal, and definite control of these scale formations with their inherent qualities is possible.

Although shifting modes are effective on a stationary key center, much melodic reference must be made to the tonic if one wishes to stay within the mode; otherwise the tonality will switch to major under the ionic power of the tritone. Melodic circling or chant-like repetition of the tonic tone and frequent cadences will help maintain the center. The following is a melody with a crescendo in register, dynamics, rhythm, and modal materials; the tonic center is A throughout.

Ex. 2-10

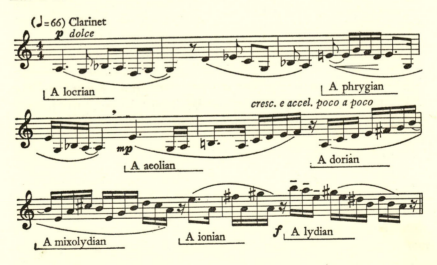

Chromatic alterations, both melodic and harmonic, are devices natural to modal writing.

Ex. 2-11

The diminished triad is a frequent subject for chromatic alteration. This chord has a restless tendency because of its tritone and is altered to give the tritone perfect-fifth stability and resonance; the root is lowered or the diminished fifth raised. This dissonant-textured diminished triad is found on a different scale step in each mode. In phrygian it occurs on the fifth scale step, and when altered, forms an additional dominant equivalent (three in all).

Ex. 2-12

In locrian, the diminished triad occurs on the tonic, but if this diminished tonic is altered chromatically in order to avoid tritone involvement with the key center chord, the locrian flavor is lessened. Therefore the tonic of this mode is often sounded with no fifth, or with an added note. The use of first inversion subdues the tritone and the omission of the third and fifth in a total unison obliterates it.

Ex. 2-13

It may be observed that since the locrian tonic triad contains the unstable tritone, melodic use may be made of the chords on the first and fifth scale steps and the tritone relationship considered a thematic characteristic.

Ex. 2-14

A pure modal passage is one in which a modal melody is harmonized with chords from the same mode and on the same tonal center.

Ex. 2-15

Polymodality involves two or more different modes on the same or different tonal centers. The modal strands may be melodic or harmonic.

Ex. 2-16

When the same mode occurs simultaneously on different tonal centers, the passage is polytonal and modal, but not polymodal.

Ex. 2-17

When different modes occur on different tonal centers at the same time the passage is both polymodal and polytonal.

Ex. 2-18

A melody may move from one mode to another with a different tonal center. If a melody fluctuates through several modes the harmony may follow with the same or with a different set of modes. When the same mode is moved from one tonal center to another a modal modulation exists,

Ex. 2-19

but when the modes change while the tonal center remains, modal interchanges result.

Ex. 2-20

In twentieth-century music, key signatures are seldom used because tonal centers and modality shift rapidly and because atonality is often present. The enharmonic choice of spelling is determined by the ease of readability.

Source Material

Dorian writing:

Ernest Bloch, Concerto Grosso No. 1, p. 1 (Birchard)
Claude Debussy, Pelléas et Mélisande (red.), p. 116 (Durand)
Roy Harris, American Ballads, p. 6 (C. Fischer)
Ottorino Respighi, Concerto Gregoriano, p. 9 (Universal)
Erik Satie, Socrate (red.), p. 35 (Sirène)
Jean Sibelius, Symphony No. 6, pp. 3–4 (Hansen)

Phrygian writing:

Ernest Bloch, Visions et Prophéties (piano), p. 10 (G. Schirmer)
Carlos Chávez, Piano Preludes, p. 3 (G. Schirmer)
Claude Debussy, String Quartet, p. 3 (Kalmus)
Goffredo Petrassi, Salmo IX (red.), p. 51 (Ricordi)
Ildebrando Pizzetti, Sonata in F for Cello and Piano, p. 16 (Ricordi)
Dmitri Shostakovich, Symphony No. 5, p. 4 (Musicus)

Lydian writing:

Benjamin Britten, Seven Sonnets of Michelangelo, p. 14 (Boosey)
Roy Harris, String Quartet No. 3, p. 10 (Mills)
Gianfrancesco Malipiero, Rispetti e Strambotti, pp. 4, 8 (Chester)
Darius Milhaud, Protée (red.), p. 1 (Durand)
Maurice Ravel, Trois Chansons, p. 12 (Durand)
Jean Sibelius, Symphony No. 4, p. 14 (Breitkopf)

Mixolydian writing:

Béla Bartók, Piano Concerto No. 3 (red.), p. 3 (Boosey)
Benjamin Britten, Serenade Op. 31, p. 1 (Boosey)
George Gershwin, Preludes for Piano, p. 5 (Harms)
Darius Milhaud, Les Songes (red.), p. 13 (Deiss)
Erik Satie, Gymnopédie No. 2 (Marks)
Dag Wiren, Serenade for String Orchestra, p. 2 (Gehrmans)

Aeolian writing:

Domingo Santa Cruz, Three Madrigals, p. 3 (Peer)
Luis Escobar, Piano Sonatine No. 2, p. 9 (Peer)
Carl Orff, Carmina Burana, p. 1 (Schott)
Ottorino Respighi, Pines of Rome, p. 34 (Ricordi)
Randall Thompson, The Peaceable Kingdom, p. 34 (E. C. Schirmer)
Virgil Thomson, Four Saints in Three Acts (red.), p. 90 (Arrow)
William Walton, Façade, p. 81 (Oxford)

Locrian writing:

Béla Bartók, Mikrokosmos Vol. II, p. 28 (Boosey)
Carlos Chávez, Preludes for Piano, pp. 5, 16 (G. Schirmer)
Claude Debussy, Sonata for Flute, Viola, and Harp, p. 11 (Durand)
Klaus Egge, Symphony No. 1, p. 6 (Lyche)
Paul Hindemith, Ludus Tonalis, p. 4 (Schott)
Goffredo Petrassi, Magnificat (red.), p. 76 (Ricordi)
Jean Sibelius, Symphony No. 4, p. 37 (Breitkopf)

Modal interchange:

Alfredo Casella, 11 Pezzi Infantili, p. 12 (Universal)
Paul Hindemith, Das Marienleben (1948), p. 18 (Schott)
Zoltán Kodály, Sonata for Solo Cello, p. 5 (Universal)
Darius Milhaud, Le Pauvre Matelot (red.), p. 1 (Heugel)
Vincent Persichetti, Piano Sonatinas, pp. 18–19 (Elkan-Vogel)
Bernard Rogers, Characters from Hans Christian Andersen, pp. 4–5 (Elkan-Vogel)

Ned Rorem, A Christmas Carol, pp. 3–5 (Elkan-Vogel)
Igor Stravinsky, L'Histoire du Soldat, pp. 59–60 (Philharmonia)

Polymodality:

Béla Bartók, String Quartet No. 3, p. 10 (Boosey)
Carlos Chávez, Sonatina for Violin and Piano, p. 4 (New Music)
Paul Hindemith, Nobilissima Visione (ballet), p. 4 (Schott)
Arthur Honegger, Sept Pièces Brèves, p. 4 (Eschig)
Olivier Messiaen, Vingt Regards (piano), p. 18 (Durand)
Darius Milhaud, Protée (red.), p. 56 (Durand)
Carl Orff, Die Bernauerin (red.), p. 85 (Schott)
Francis Poulenc, Mouvements Perpetuels, p. 2 (Chester)
Maurice Ravel, Piano Concerto in G (red.), p. 38 (Durand)
Igor Stravinsky, Oedipus Rex (red.), p. 79 (Russe)

SYNTHETIC SCALE FORMATIONS

Although a single tone, through its overtone series, suggests most obviously the major scale, the formation is partly rationalized. The major is only one of many scales contained in the basic twelve-tone chromatic scale that is found in the upper region of the overtone series. Free placement of scale steps results in original scale formations beyond the sphere of major and minor modes.

Most original scales are constructed by placing any number of major, minor, and augmented seconds in any order. The permutation possibilities are staggering and the mathematical process has little creative connection with composition. It is advisable that scales be allowed to form as a result of the impetus of melodic or harmonic patterns; the material generated by thematic ideas may then be gathered up and placed into scale formation.

Some "original" or synthetic scales are used more often than others. These better-known scales often coincide with folk scales and are sometimes named as follows:

Ex. 2-21

The synthetic seven-tone, one-octave scale, like a major or minor, is made of a pair of four-note groups (tetrachords) that repeat the tonic at the eighth step. These tetrachords may be similar, as in major and Double Harmonic scales, or different, as in harmonic minor and Hungarian Major scales.

The modal construction principle that produced the seven diatonic modes (dorian, phrygian, etc.) may be applied to any scale, creating multiple versions. The first modal version of any scale begins on the tonic, the second on the supertonic of that scale, etc.

Ex. 2-22

The harmonic usefulness of new scales is determined by survey-
ing their indigenous chordal materials. Each synthetic scale contains a set of chords within its own intervallic make-up. The
primary chords are the tonic plus the two triads that include the
scale step or steps containing the most determinable characteristic
colors of the scale in question. If a major-scale tetrachord is present
the color tones are those outside the tetrachord. But if the scale
contains no major-key tetrachord, the primary chords other than
the tonic are those triads that are enharmonic spellings of a major
or minor triad. If enharmonically spelled major or minor triads
do not exist, the characteristic tone or tones are found in the notes
forming augmented or diminished intervals with the tonic. The remaining triads are the secondary formations that function within
the gravitation of the primary chords.

Ex. 2-23

A harmonic problem is created by the fact that most synthetic scales produce one or more triads with diminished or augmented thirds and often these triads are primaries. They are usually chromatically converted into one of the four basic triads: major, minor, augmented, or diminished. Altering the harmonic texture should not disturb the strict scale tones in the melodic writing because the burden of maintaining the flavor of the prevailing scale is placed upon the melody. The sooner the melodic voice includes all the tones of the scale, the greater the chance of projecting the synthetic scale as a unit.

Ex. 2-24

Further harmonic possibilities may be tested by considering the mirrored version of the scale. Scanning intervallic points between the original and mirrored versions reveals hidden potentialities of the scale. Fresh material such as cadential patterns, passing textures, and outer-voice movement is suggested and brought into focus by reflection.

Ex. 2-25

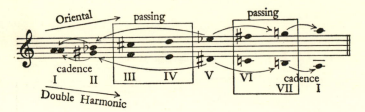

Some scales are reflectively identical, inversion producing an exact duplication of the original scale in retrograde.

Ex. 2-26

As in previously discussed modal writing, the melody and harmony of a passage involving synthetic scales may stem from the same scale or different scales, and be placed on identical or different key centers. The following passage is built of different scales on the same tonal center:

Ex. 2-27

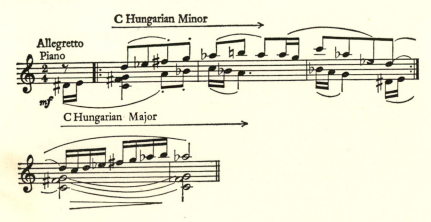

This next passage is built of different scales on different tonal centers:

Ex. 2-28

New scales may be so built with similar or dissimilar tetrachords that the tonic is not repeated at the first octave. When the octave is missed and the tetrachords are continued, a two-octave scale or multi-octave scale may evolve.

Ex. 2-29

A second type of two-octave scale is built by combining two different one-octave scales with common tonics.

Ex. 2-30

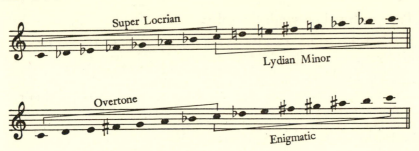

Tones 9 through 15 of a two-octave scale are not necessarily duplications of tones 2 through 8. This tremendous span of intervallic color makes shifting of modal versions impracticable. The principal chords of the two-octave scale tend to be large, complex structures which clearly define the two-octave compass. The fifteenth and seventeenth of a chord by thirds from the two-octave scale are not necessarily duplications of the root and third. These two-octave scales serve as a unifying element in music of complex chordal formations.

Ex. 2-31

Built on 2-8ve scale   (Ex. 2-29)

Two or more tonal levels of intricate two-octave formations appearing at the same time (polymodal or polytonal) are difficult to project, and are best contained in music for a medium of wide color palette.

Source Material

Passages based on synthetic scales:

Béla Bartók, Sonata for Two Pianos and Percussion, p. 65 (Boosey)
Niels Viggo Bentzon, Third Piano Sonata, p. 17 (Hansen)
Benjamin Britten, Turn of the Screw (red.), p. 180 (Boosey)
Ross Lee Finney, Piano Quintet, p. 33 (U. of Mich.)
Charles Griffes, The Pleasure-Dome of Kubla Khan, p. 14 (G. Schirmer)
Lou Harrison, Suite for Cello and Harp, p. 10 (Peer)
Arthur Honegger, Symphony No. 5, p. 49 (Salabert)
Alan Hovhaness, Lousnag Kisher, pp. 2–5 (Merion)
Olivier Messiaen, Vingt Regards (piano), p. 128 (Durand)
Goffredo Petrassi, Magnificat (red.), p. 86 (Ricordi)
Manuel M. Ponce, 3 Poemas de Lermontow, p. 6 (Universidad, Argentina)
Maurice Ravel, Concerto for Left Hand (red.), p. 20 (Durand)
Harald Saeverud, Siljuslåtten, p. 5 (Norsk)
Jean Sibelius, Symphony No. 4, p. 13 (Breitkopf)
Igor Stravinsky, Fire-Bird Suite, p. 25 (Kalmus)

PENTATONIC AND HEXATONIC SCALES

There are various kinds of basic five-tone or pentatonic scales. Some of the better known are:

Ex. 2-32

The modal construction technique that produces the seven diatonic modes produces five modes of each type of pentatonic scale. The five modal forms of the diatonic pentatonic are as follows:

Ex. 2-33

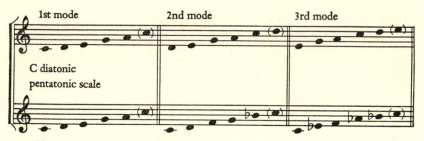

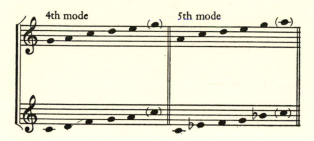

Transposed to same tonic for comparison

Diatonic scales of five tones are harmonically limited in scope because of the lack of semitones (when all five tones of a pentatonic scale are sounded together they form a somewhat static chord). It is therefore extremely difficult to achieve harmonic and melodic direction in a pure pentatonic form.

When melody and harmony are pentatonic, changing the modal versions of the pentatonic or moving from one pentatonic to another will help prevent monotony.

Ex. 2-34

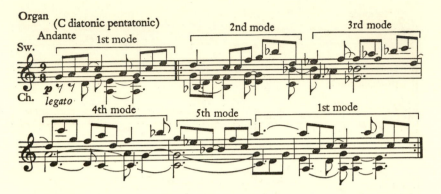

Lavish use of ornamental tones, pedal points, and frequent modal interchanges or modulations to other pentatonics will also help prevent harmonic monotony; but pure pentatonic music (non-polymodal, etc.) is most effective when used for short spans of time. Pentatonic materials function well melodically or harmonically, but seldom both. Pentatonic melodies are often harmonized with foreign chords.

Ex. 2-35

One type of pentatonic scale combines well with another type on the same or different key centers.

Ex. 2-36

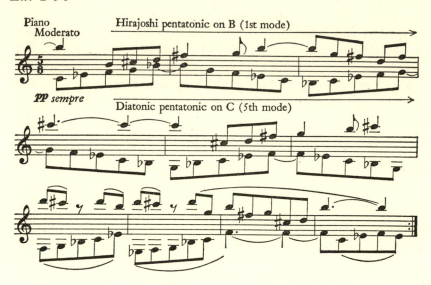

There are various kinds of basic six-tone or hexatonic scales. Some of the better known are:

Ex. 2-37

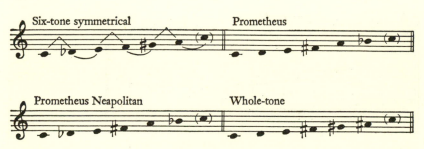

The modal construction technique that produces the seven diatonic modes and the five modes of the pentatonics, produces six modes of each type of hexatonic scale except the whole-tone scale. Harmonic monotony is somewhat more easily avoided in pure hexatonic scales than it is in pentatonic scales because of the additional interval. Melodic material from these scales is usually harmonized with chords from other scales or with chords in non-scalar relationship.

The hexatonic scale (excepting the whole-tone) has a primarily melodic function. When it is used as material for melodic writing a complete and fully independent line evolves. At times the harmony is drawn into the tonal orbit of the melody, but for the most part the harmony is non-hexatonic and moves independent of any implications of the melody. The consonant-dissonant tension caused by the two separate forces creates its own fluctuating design and shape. In hexatonic passages the two strong forces, melody and harmony, are often in polytonal relationship.

Ex. 2-38

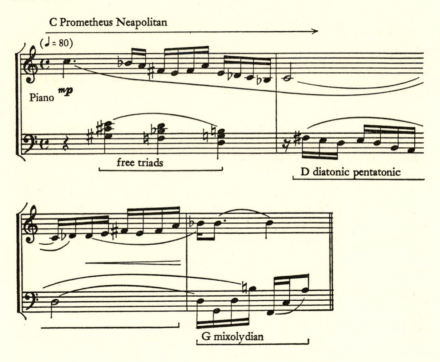

The whole-tone hexatonic scale offers a limited basis for extended musical expression. When the scale is mirrored there is no change except in register. A second whole-tone scale lies a half step above a first but any attempt to produce more will result not only in a transposition but in a duplication of the notes of the first or second. Modal versions of either of the two scales result in an exact transposition of the original forms. Its equidistant intervallic make-up deprives the scale of the fundamental intervals, the perfect fourth and fifth, and of the leading tone. A real feeling of tonality, therefore, must be established by harmony outside the whole-tone category.

The chords furnished by the whole-tone hexatonic scale are meager harmonic material. The six triads of the scale are all augmented and four of them are, in effect, but inversions of the first two. There is only one type of seventh, one type of ninth chord, and one category of chords by seconds.

Ex. 2-39

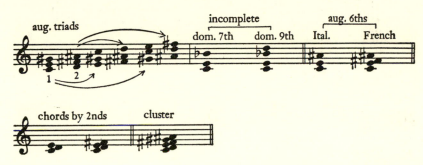

Nevertheless, whole-tone materials have possibilities when certain devices are employed to prolong the harmonic interest. These are:

contrary motion,

Ex. 2-40

alternating the two scales,

Ex. 2-41

sounding all six tones together harmonically,

Ex. 2-42

changing the density and spacing,

Ex. 2-43

and using both whole-tone scales simultaneously.

Ex. 2-44

The true value of the whole-tone scale lies in the contrast it provides when it is used in combination with other scales and techniques. When amalgamated with other materials it can be creatively stimulating, as in:

a whole-tone melody harmonized with chords other than whole-tone,

Ex. 2-45

a diatonic melody created over whole-tone harmony,

Ex. 2-46

whole-tone chords changed to added-note chords when minor
seconds are attached,

Ex. 2-47

whole-tone passages alternated with non-whole-tone passages,

Ex. 2-48

and the whole-tone scale combined with another kind of scale.

Ex. 2-49

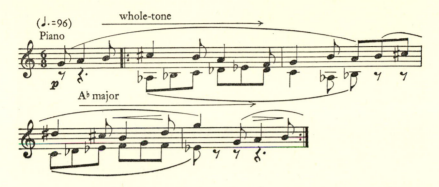

Source Material

Pentatonic writing:

Béla Bartók, Mikrokosmos Vol. III, p. 22 (Boosey)
Claude Debussy, Preludes Vol. I, p. 16 (Durand)
Charles Griffes, Five Poems of the Ancient Far East (voice and piano),
    pp. 4–15 (G. Schirmer)
Gianfrancesco Malipiero, Pause del Silenzio, p. 37 (Philharmonia)
Maurice Ravel, Trio for Violin, Cello, and Piano, p. 21 (Durand)
Albert Roussel, Douze Mélodies (voice and piano), p. 49 (Lerolle)

Pentatonic and non-pentatonic combinations:

Béla Bartók, String Quartet No. 3, pp. 7–8 (Boosey)
Paul Hindemith, Tanzstücke (piano), p. 18 (Schott)
Arthur Honegger, Trois Chansons, p. 2 (Senart)
Burrill Phillips, A Set of Three Informalities for Piano, p. 4 (G. Schirmer)
Maurice Ravel, L'Enfant et les Sortilèges, pp. 42–43 (Durand)
Ralph Vaughan Williams, A London Symphony, p. 24 (Stainer)

Whole-tone writing:

Béla Bartók, Mikrokosmos Vol. V, p. 32 (Boosey)
Alban Berg, Sieben Frühe Lieder, p. 3 (Universal)
Claude Debussy, Preludes Vol. I, p. 3 (Durand)
Paul Hindemith, Neues vom Tage (red.), p. 171 (Schott)

Whole-tone and non-whole-tone combinations:

Béla Bartók, String Quartet No. 1, p. 11 (Boosey)
Ferruccio Busoni, Piano Sonatina No. 1, p. 11 (Zimmermann)
Paul Hindemith, Piano Sonata No. 1, p. 15 (Schott)
Jacques Ibert, Angélique (red.), p. 24 (Heugel)
Charles Ives, Thirty-four Songs (Mists), p. 46 (New Music)
Maurice Ravel, Ma Mère l'Oye (4 hands), pp. 18–19 (Durand)
Igor Stravinsky, Le Sacre du Printemps, p. 67 (Kalmus)

THE CHROMATIC SCALE

The chromatic scale is made of the octave divided into twelve half steps. It is used as an ornamentation of a diatonic scale, or as an independent scale (dodecuple) with twelve equally important steps. This chromatic scale may impose tonic feeling through fixed or shifting centers or may have no definite tonality. Modal versions in the equidistant chromatic scale are no more possible to construct than in the equidistant whole-tone scale.

However, chords of equidistant intervals or any combination of mixed intervals may be built from the scale. They may be constructed upon any or all chromatic tones and, if desired, brought within the gravitation of a tonic center through establishment of any plan of chordal relationships. Chromatic harmony often contains miscellaneous intervallic building materials. This complex harmony forms a compound type that is discussed in a later chapter.

There are various kinds of chromatic writing:

chromatic figuration of non-chromatic harmony,

Ex. 2-50

chromatic harmony with diatonic melodic writing,

Ex. 2-51

chromatic melody generated by chromatic harmony,

Ex. 2-52

mixed chordal structures formed by the chromatic motion of parts,

Ex. 2-53

and chromatic harmony generated by chromatic melodic writing.

Ex. 2-54

    When characteristic groups of melodic notes are used vertically, as above, chords are formed by intervals from the horizontal motif. Composition with twelve notes can generate this kind of harmony.

Source Material

Chromatic figuration of non-chromatic harmony:

Henry Cowell, Symphony No. 11, p. 15 (Associated)
Arthur Honegger, King David (red.), p. 6 (Foetisch)
Serge Prokofiev, Piano Sonata No. 2, p. 3 (Leeds)
Dmitri Shostakovich, Piano Prelude No. 1 (Leeds)
Igor Stravinsky, Symphony of Psalms (red.), p. 2 (Boosey)

Chromatic harmony with diatonic melody:

Samuel Barber, Piano Sonata, p. 42 (G. Schirmer)
Roy Harris, Little Suite, p. 5 (G. Schirmer)
Paul Hindemith, Sonata for Piano, Four Hands, pp. 10–11 (Schott)
Charles Ives, Violin Sonata No. 4, p. 19 (Arrow)

Chromatic harmony with chromatic melody:

Alban Berg, Fünf Orchester-Lieder, Op. 4 (red.), p. 5 (Universal)
Bruno Bettinelli, Sinfonia Breve, p. 52 (Ricordi)
Gottfried von Einem, Japanische Blätter, p. 2 (Universal)
Howard Hanson, Symphony No. 2, p. 2 (C. Fischer)
Carl Ruggles, Men and Mountains, p. 15 (New Music)
Arnold Schoenberg, Violin Concerto (red.), p. 33 (G. Schirmer)
Alexander Scriabine, Piano Sonata No. 9, p. 1 (Leeds)
Roger Sessions, Piano Concerto (red.), p. 34 (Marks)

Applications

1. Write a short piano piece in the mixolydian mode, with a minimum of chromatic alteration.

2. Extend these opening string quartet measures using the lydian mode.

Ex. 2-55

3. Write a passage for organ employing modal modulation.

4. Write a passage for harp illustrating modal interchange.

5. Write a short recitative for violin using fluctuating modes.

6. Write a gay and quickly moving vocalise for soprano based upon the darker modes.

7. Write a slow and melancholy vocalise for baritone employing only bright modes.

8. Construct a solo clarinet line in the lydian mode supported by

phrygian string-quartet harmony. Set both the melody and harmony on the tonal center B♭.

9. Move a woodwind quintet rapidly through a section of mostly mixolydian music.

10. Harmonize a locrian English horn melody with locrian divisi cello harmony on the same center.

11. Extend the following polymodal and polytonal passage.

Ex. 2-56

12. Write original melodies for various instruments using original scales.

13. Write a one-voice fantasy for organ, pedals alone, using several synthetic or original scales.

14. Construct a canon for three clarinets in which each performer plays a different synthetic scale on a different tonic.

15. Create an original two-octave-scale harmonic texture in a scherzino for piano, four hands.

16. Write a purely pentatonic section of a scherzo for woodwind quintet.

17. Allow an oboe to sing a slow pentatonic line over a non-pentatonic chordal string background.

18. Move the orchestra quickly through a florid passage based upon shifting pentatonic scales.

19. Construct two melodies on a whole-tone scale, one suitable for the theme of a lyric movement and the other for the theme of a scherzo movement.

20. Harmonize a descending whole-tone scale in the tuba with major and minor triads in the trumpet, horn, and trombone.

21. Harmonize an ascending major scale with various kinds of whole-tone materials. Use any medium.

22. Pit high brasses (using one whole-tone scale) against low brasses (using the other whole-tone scale).

23. Write a chromatic bassoon melody under three-part diatonic string harmony.

24. Extend the following chromatically ornamented piano passage.

Ex. 2-57

25. Harmonize an ascending chromatic scale in the soprano saxophone, with major and minor triads in an alto and two tenor saxophones.

Chords by Thirds

TRIADS

TRIADS ARE USED by composers of the twentieth century in ways
not emphasized in the eighteenth and nineteenth centuries. Chords
of the earlier period revolve around the tonal pillars—tonic,
dominant, and subdominant—and gravitation is created by the
anticipation of harmonic arrival. The dominant and subdominant
balance the tonic on either side in intervals of the fifth, and these
relationships (V-I and IV-I) dominate all others. The remaining
chords are secondary and furnish variety once the primary color
has been established. The motion to and from the primary material
gives the key its identity and the music its balance. Since this
dominant-subdominant harmony is used for cadential feeling, the
progression is unquestionably established as being governed by a
fifth relationship or a cycle of fifths.

Ex. 3-1

IV I V (5⁺)

Triadic materials within a scale may be set in motion by relationships other than that of the fifth. In their music composers
have shown that, as it is possible to have a cycle of fifths, so it is
possible to move in a cycle of thirds or seconds. These relationships
can be convincing to the ear when the cycle in force is confirmed
by passing and cadential chordal movements. In third relationship
(cycle of thirds) the mediant and submediant give balanced support to the tonic from their positions a third above and below the
tonic. The primary chords then are I, III, and VI and those remaining are secondary. The relationships III-I and VI-I dominate all
others.

Ex. 3-2

VI I III (5⁺)

In second relationship (cycle of seconds) the supertonic and
leading-tone chords help establish the tonic center from their positions a second in either direction. Primary chords are I, II, and
VII and the remaining chords secondary. The relationships II-I
and VII-I dominate the others.

Ex. 3-3

VII I II
(5⁺)

When determining the succession of chords in a third or second
relationship one may proceed in their equivalent of the traditional
fifth relationship of roots. The most natural root progressions of
the second and third relationships parallel the usual root progres-

sions in music based upon the cycle of fifths. Here are corresponding chords of all categories, their tonal functions (cadential,
modulatory, and so on) being parallel:

$$
\begin{array}{llll}
\text{Cycle of} & \text{5ths} & \text{3rds} & \text{2nds} \\
\text{IV} & = \text{VI} & = \text{VII} \\
\text{VII} & = \text{IV} & = \text{VI} \\
\text{III} & = \text{II} & = \text{V} \\
\text{VI} & = \text{VII} & = \text{IV} \\
\text{II} & = \text{V} & = \text{III} \\
\text{V} & = \text{III} & = \text{II} \\
\text{I} & = \text{I} & = \text{I}
\end{array}
$$

and corresponding harmonic progressions:

$$
\begin{array}{llllllll}
\text{Cycle of 5ths} & \text{I} & \text{III} & \text{IV} & \text{VI} & \text{V} & \text{I} \\
\text{Cycle of 3rds} & \text{I} & \text{II} & \text{VI} & \text{VII} & \text{III} & \text{I} \\
\text{Cycle of 2nds} & \text{I} & \text{V} & \text{VII} & \text{IV} & \text{II} & \text{I}
\end{array}
$$

In the following example the root progression is created by
descending in successive intervals of the cycle relationship in force.
Here the passages are different only in that they are governed by
different cycles—fifths, thirds, and seconds.

Ex. 3-4

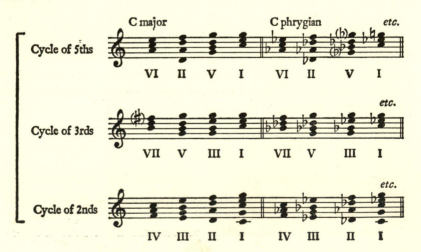

These cyclic relationships may be constructed in any scale, synthetic or otherwise. In a major key the primary chords in a fifth relationship are major, in aeolian they are minor, and in many synthetic scales they are mixed. In second and third relationships, as in the fifth, the colors of primary chords are determined by the intervallic make-up of the scale in force and will vary considerably.

A third relationship in a major key produces the following harmonic colors in primary chords: I major, III minor, and VI minor. There are major as well as minor secondary chords, these triads creating useful color tension in a secondary chordal function. In this context a C major E-G-B "dominant" is as refreshing as the secondary G-B-D.

Ex. 3-5

In modes, the primary chords of a particular cyclic relationship may not coincide with the natural modal primary chords explained in Chapter 2. For example, a second relationship in the phrygian happens to include the natural primary chords of the mode (I, II, and VII). The dominant equivalents, II and VII, contain the characteristic phrygian second scale step. A third relationship in phrygian produces the primary triads I, III, and VI, but these chords do not include the phrygian flavor tone. Even though the phrygian sound is difficult to capture under these circumstances, it is quite possible to establish this third relationship by emphasis upon the secondary chords of the cycle which do contain the phrygian color.

Ex. 3-6

The harmonic motion to and from primary chords may change to a motion created by shifting from one cycle to another. Interchange of the three relationships (second, third, and fifth) affords complete freedom of root movement within a scale. Every intervallic root progression is possible because movements of the second, third, and fifth are identical to those of the seventh, sixth, and fourth by inversion. And since the intervals between moving roots appear as major, minor, perfect, and augmented (depending upon the scale in use), the whole twelve-tone compass of intervallic root progression is automatically available.

To find ornamental tones, any chord of the harmonic progression may be considered a "tonic" of any scale, synthetic or otherwise, and ornamental tones may be derived from that inferred scale.

Ex. 3-7

Synthetic scales often contain triads that have augmented or diminished thirds. These are awkward because they sound like fourths or seconds and usually result in misspelling a chord.

Ex. 3-8

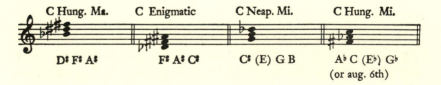

Such chords are often altered to one of the four basic triads, major, minor, diminished, or augmented, in which only major and minor thirds are present.

Chords may move as part of a cycle within a scale, or independent of scale relationship in triads built upon any tone. In music that lacks a definite scale or modality, any triad may be followed by any other triad and any sequence of key centers may be used. The root movement of a perfect fifth has a strong tendency to establish a definite modality and tonality, and therefore is seldom used in a chromatically free triadic context. Root movements of major and minor seconds and major and minor thirds occur more often because they are less likely to define any one scale, the root of one triad moving up or down to the root of another triad more often in intervals of seconds and thirds than in fifths or the tritone. Both triads involved may be of any type, but are usually major or minor.

Ex. 3-9

C E♭ D F♯ A B♭ C

When triads progress chromatically a root movement of the augmented fourth produces a chordal relationship that adds variety to the basic second-third relationship.

Ex. 3-10

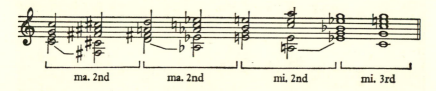

ma. 2nd   ma. 2nd   mi. 2nd   mi. 3rd

The wide selection of triads made available by chromatic progression often creates harmonic and tonal restlessness. But if each voice has purpose and design any triad may progress freely and with harmonic meaning. When chromatic triads wander harmonically and make vague phrase-shapes a diatonic melody may bring the chromaticism into clear focus.

Ex. 3-11

At any point chordal material may be chosen by considering a prominent note in the strongest voice as the root, third, or fifth of a major or minor (less often, diminished or augmented) triad. Any note has three major and three minor triadic possibilities.

Ex. 3-12

Even an unadorned scale line produces potential chordal variety.

Ex. 3-13

In music of such chromatic shifting, an underlying scale or mode is sometimes a resultant factor but never a governing one. Although the center of the following example is indisputably F, the passage is not governed by a prevailing mode or a preconceived tonal framework.

Ex. 3-14

Triads are frequently used in fundamental position while the voices containing the root and fifth (usually the two bottom voices) move in parallel fifths. This type of movement is effective if attention is diverted from the fifths by extensive contrary motion. Periodic inversion of the triads will relieve the binding parallelism.

Ex. 3-15

In the last chord of the above example, the minor six-three functions as an incomplete major triad with an added sixth (F♯ tonic).

The six-four chord with its characteristic interval of a fourth is often heard in the company of simple chords by fourths. The mild tension of the second inversion and the punctuation of recurring cadences help define the formal arc of longer triadic passages. In these surroundings modal cadences of second and third relationships find their natural habitat.

Source Material

Triads moving by third relationship:

Samuel Barber, Dover Beach (red.), p. 12 (G. Schirmer)
Benjamin Britten, Piano Concerto (red.), p. 46 (Boosey)
Frank Martin, Golgotha (red.), p. 12 (Universal)
Serge Prokofiev, March from L'Amour des Trois Oranges (Breitkopf)
William Schuman, Symphony No. 4, pp. 34–35 (G. Schirmer)
Virgil Thomson, A Solemn Music, for band (red.), p. 7 (G. Schirmer)

Triads moving by second relationship:

Samuel Barber, Adagio for Strings, p. 3 (G. Schirmer)
Aaron Copland, Clarinet Concerto (red.), p. 2 (Boosey)
Arthur Honegger, King David (red.), p. 15 (Chester)
Douglas Moore, The Ballad of Baby Doe (red.), p. 155 (Chappell)
Serge Prokofiev, Classical Symphony, p. 51 (Baron)
Erik Satie, Socrate (red.), p. 15 (Sirène)

Triads moving by tritone relationship:

Dominick Argento, The Boor (red.), p. 29 (Boosey)
Béla Bartók, Violin Sonata No. 1, p. 21 (Universal)
Alan Hovhaness, Mysterious Mountain, p. 64 (Associated)
Gian Carlo Menotti, Amahl and the Night Visitors (red.), p. 21 (G. Schirmer)
Willem Pijper, Piano Sonatina No. 3, p. 6 (Oxford)
Erik Satie, Sonneries de la Rose + Croix, p. 7 (Lerolle)

SEVENTH AND NINTH CHORDS

The seventh and ninth members of chords are traditionally dissonant tones but they have been freed of some of their former restrictions. These chords have become stable entities in themselves with their dissonant tones not necessarily prepared or resolved. Seventh and ninth chords, like triads, may progress within or outside any scale formation, original or traditional. Under certain formal conditions the seventh and ninth are treated as dissonant tones needing resolution; but as independent seventh and ninth chords they have the facility of triads.

Ex. 3-16

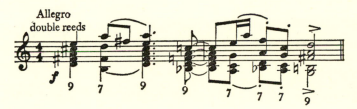

It is possible to build seven different seventh chords with major and minor third construction. Seventh chords with augmented and diminished thirds are misspellings of other chords.

Ex. 3-17

Great variety in seventh chord texture can be had through doubling (any note may be doubled) and inversion. Sevenths may be inverted and spaced in any manner without destroying their harmonic suppleness. The first inversion, spaced in fifths, is particularly useful because its unique sound enables it to act as a key center chord.

Ex. 3-18

All types of harmonic progression possible with triads are possible with seventh and ninth chords. Seventh and ninth chords used as consonant formations function well in relationships established by a cycle of fifths, thirds, or seconds. The augmented fourth root relationship provides fresh activity from chord to chord, particularly when the chords are dominant sevenths.

Ex. 3-19

A feeling of "progression" may be created by moving voices through various forms of different seventh and ninth formations on the same root.

Ex. 3-20

Mathematically, it should be possible to build with major and minor thirds sixteen different ninth chords on one note; but because of enharmonic duplication of certain notes, only twelve are possible. For scanning purposes the ninth chord is analyzed as consisting of two triads, the top triad anchored to the uppermost note of the bottom triad. This dual chording has polychordal implications.

Ex. 3-21

A workable order of the twelve ninth chords from darkest to brightest is material for a composer's craft (the chords connected by arrows may be interchanged).

Ex. 3-22

When color gradations of the ninth formations are made part of the composer's aural apparatus, textural control of the various ninth chords will be possible. Ninths used with technical facility add freshness to harmonic progression.

Ex. 3-23

One of the thirds that makes up a ninth chord may be (but rarely is) smaller than a minor third. The harmonic squeeze caused by the diminished third, or its inversion the augmented sixth, creates a need for chromatic resolution.

Ex. 3-24

In ninth chords members are omitted as follows: fifth—for richness; third or seventh—for less color. Chord members are doubled as follows: root or fifth—for solidity; third or seventh—for density of color; ninth—for increased tension.

When the ninth of the chord is below the root the chord is less agile; fluent part-writing helps the progression.

Ex. 3-25

The fourth inversion (ninth in the bass) is a hard texture and effective in a rough-hewn passage. Omitting the fifth here produces more suppleness.

Ex. 3-26

The minor dominant ninth in the fourth inversion is often found with its seventh omitted in parallel harmony. In fourth inversion the interval of the minor ninth is sometimes spelled as a diminished octave to facilitate reading.

Ex. 3-27

Extensive materials are made available by ninth formations. Since any note may be considered the root, third, fifth, seventh, or ninth of twelve different ninth chords, a single tone may be harmonized with sixty different ninths. With the note E in the top voice, the five minor-minor ninth chords might be written:

Ex. 3-28

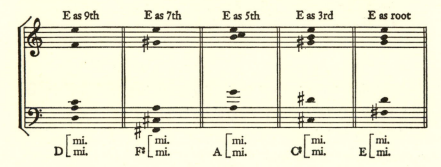

Successions of ninths of varying intervallic textures are effective in sequential patterns,

Ex. 3-29

and in combination with sevenths.

Ex. 3-30

The increased harmonic weight of ninths often presents the problem of immobility. This may be solved by merely touching the ninth with a voice moving from a triad or seventh chord.

Ex. 3-31

When ninth chords are used with chords by fourths or other non-third categories the members of the ninth are spaced so that at least one of the intervals of this chord resembles the building interval of the non-tertian harmony. For example, if ninth chords are followed by chords built of fourths, the members of the ninth are arranged so that an interval of the fourth is formed by two of the voices. This fourth is given emphasis in the phrase to prepare the texture for the entrance of the chord by fourths. Progressions that combine chordal textures are, however, a matter for study under Harmonic Synthesis; see Chapter 13.

Source Material

Various kinds of seventh and ninth chords:

Alban Berg, Piano Sonata, p. 10 (Universal)
Paul Creston, Symphony No. 2, p. 5 (G. Schirmer)
Klaus Egge, Symphony No. 1, p. 74 (Lyche)
Lukas Foss, The Jumping Frog (red.), pp. 84–85 (C. Fischer)
George Gershwin, Porgy and Bess (red.), p. 8 (Chappell)
Roy Harris, Soliloquy and Dance, for viola and piano, p. 4 (G. Schirmer)
Charles Ives, Walking (Arrow)
Goffredo Petrassi, Magnificat (red.), p. 56 (Ricordi)
Maurice Ravel, Valses Nobles et Sentimentales, p. 3 (Durand)
Erik Satie, Sarabande No. 2 (Lerolle)
Arnold Schoenberg, Six Little Piano Pieces, Op. 19, p. 4 (Associated)
Alexander Scriabine, Piano Sonata No. 5, p. 16 (International)
Igor Stravinsky, Threni (red.), p. 44 (Boosey)
Guido Turchi, Preludi e Fughette per Pianoforte, p. 3 (Zerboni)

ELEVENTHS AND THIRTEENTHS

Large tertian chords, no matter how many thirds have been added, form only a small portion of the harmonic palette. The multiple tones of eleventh and thirteenth chords add density but reduce suppleness. These six- and seven-note formations are cumbersome in harmonic progressions but useful in the general harmonic scheme.

An eleventh chord is easily identified by considering the formation a combination of two triads a major or minor third apart.

Ex. 3-32

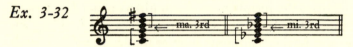

A thirteenth chord may be identified by considering the formation a simultaneous combination of three triads with tones in common at two points.

Ex. 3-33

The thirteenth chord is non-invertible; any attempt at inversion will produce another eleventh or thirteenth.

Ex. 3-34

Eleventh and thirteenth sounds are often created by pedal tones or melodic ornamentation of triads and seventh chords. In these instances the harmonic background is not one of eleventh or thirteenth chords but a smaller chord with the addition of ornamental tones. In analysis the apparent eleventh or thirteenth is broken down to the chord with the fewest notes and this considered the basic chord; otherwise ornamental tones are mistakenly considered part of the chord.

Ex. 3-35

If some members of the eleventh and thirteenth chords are omitted it is possible to attain a certain freedom of harmonic movement. Eleventh and thirteenth chords usually contain two sharp dissonant intervals. Omitting one of the tones that forms a sharp dissonant interval lessens the dissonant content and makes relatively supple harmonic movement possible. In the following thirteenth-chord example, CB and EF are members of the sharp intervals contained in the chord. E, B, or F are choice notes of omission; if C, the root, were omitted an eleventh chord would result.

Ex. 3-36

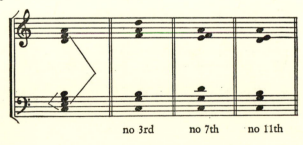

Chord members are best arranged in resonant intervallic relationship; but if the arrangement produces two separate triadic units a

polychord results; and if fourths predominate the chords sound
not as elevenths or thirteenths but as chords by fourths.

Ex. 3-37

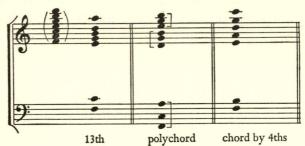

13th   polychord   chord by 4ths

The intervallic make-up of eleventh and thirteenth chords often
coincides with various scale formations,

Ex. 3-38

Super Locrian   phrygian   Overtone   Hung. Ma.   Leading
                                                              Whole-tone

and the chords become excellent six- and seven-note tonic formations around which polychords and compound structures may
function. These eleventh and thirteenth formations are usually
guided by a melodic line derived from the scale implied by the
rich tonic chord; they are seldom found in extensive part-writing.

Eleventh and thirteenth chords combine well with seventh and
ninth chords.

Ex. 3-39

Source Material

Eleventh and thirteenth chords:

Alban Berg, Wozzeck (red.), p. 39 (Universal)
Benjamin Britten, Peter Grimes (red.), p. 27 (Boosey)
Arthur Honegger, Jeanne d'Arc au Bûcher (red.), p. 84 (Salabert)
Darius Milhaud, Les Malheurs d'Orphée (red.), p. 27 (Heugel)
Walter Piston, Carnival Song (men's chorus and brasses), p. 26 (Arrow)
Maurice Ravel, Valses Nobles et Sentimentales, p. 1 (Durand)
Harold Shapero, Sonata for Piano, Four Hands, p. 9 (Affiliated)
Igor Stravinsky, Octuor, p. 52 (Boosey)
Alexander Scriabine, Piano Sonata No. 8, p. 1 (Leeds)

FIFTEENTHS AND SEVENTEENTHS

As the tonal system expanded into one that accommodated more than seven different chord tones, thirds were added to the thirteenth chord as a fifteenth and a seventeenth without duplicating chord members.

Ex. 3-40

17th   13th
         with doubling

In tertian chords larger than the seventeenth, not every tone is necessarily different; the size of the chord is determined by the distance between the root and the highest new note that rises in thirds above the root.

Ex. 3-41

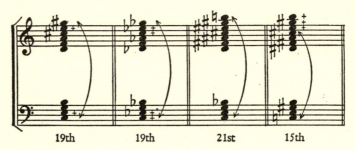

For purposes of manipulation, the texture of these large chords should be thinned by omitting two or three inner tones. Separated triadic units must be avoided unless polychordal structure is desired.

Ex. 3-42

Complete fifteenth or seventeenth chords are effective in parallel harmony or in harmonic punctuations.

Ex. 3-43

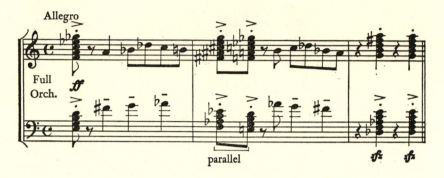

Source Material

Fifteenth and seventeenth chords:

Henk Badings, Louisville-Symphony, p. 63 (Peters)
Alban Berg, Violin Concerto (red.), p. 42 (Universal)
Arthur Honegger, Symphonie Liturgique, p. 106 (Salabert)
Charles Ives, 19 Songs (On the Antipodes), p. 44 (New Music)
Giselher Klebe, Moments Musicaux for Orchestra, p. 1 (Bote)
Riccardo Malipiero, Sonata for Violin and Piano, p. 18 (Zerboni)
Maurice Ravel, Chansons Madécasses (red.), p. 12 (Durand)
Alexandre Tansman, Quatre Préludes, p. 5 (Demets)
Heitor Villa-Lobos, Rudepoema, p. 22 (Eschig)

TWELVE-NOTE CHORDS

Mixed thirds may be superimposed until all twelve tones are present. The unwieldy terms "nineteenth," "twenty-first," or "twenty-third" chord are seldom used. Twelve-note chords containing twelve different member tones are so complex and thick that special attention must be given to the register and instrumentation. The thick texture lightens when the chord is placed in the upper register or when consonant portions of the chord are played by separate orchestral choirs.

Ex. 3-44

This is an extremely limited species of harmony, which operates in a confined area; its harmonic functions are few. Twelve-note chords are used for punctuation,

Ex. 3-45

for quiet and sustained tension,

Ex. 3-46

and for short progressions that answer unison or two-part writing.

Ex. 3-47

Twelve-note chords by thirds span a wide register and their members are normally spaced in thirds. Parallel movement of all voices provides temporary "suppleness" but when contrary motion in some voices is used the distances between some of the voices change. This results in the twelve-note chords by thirds moving to one formed by fourths or seconds, or to a polychord, heterogeneous compound chord, or mirror chord:

Ex. 3-48

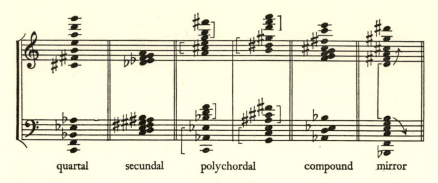

| quartal | secundal | polychordal | compound | mirror |

Source Material

Twelve-note chords:

Alban Berg, Fünf Orchester-Lieder (red.), p. 6 (Universal)
Leonard Bernstein, The Age of Anxiety (red.), p. 59 (G. Schirmer)
Karl-Birger Blomdahl, Aniara (red.), pp. 1–3 (Schott)
Benjamin Britten, The Turn of the Screw (red.), p. 5 (Boosey)
Vittorio Giannini, Symphony No. 4, III, at rehearsal number 9 (Ricordi)
Michael Gielen, Musica per Archi, Pianoforte, Baritono, Trombone, e
    Timpani, p. 39 (Universal)
Everett Helm, Concerto for Five Solo Instruments, Percussion, and Strings,
    p. 15 (Schott)
Charles Ives, 19 Songs (Majority), p. 42 (New Music)
Rolf Liebermann, Concerto for Jazz Band and Symphony Orchestra, p. 1
    (Universal)
Darius Milhaud, Piano Sonata (1916), p. 10 (Salabert)
Vincent Persichetti, Symphony for Band, p. 127 (Elkan-Vogel)
Bernard Rogers, The Passion (red.), p. 98 (Elkan-Vogel)

Applications

1. Write a dorian passage for piano in which the harmony is dominated by the cycle of fifths.

2. Set for mixed chorus a line from one of the Psalms. Let the music be governed primarily by the cycle of thirds.

3. Write a mixolydian passage for two oboes and two bassoons in which the harmony is governed by the cycle of seconds.

4. Construct a phrase on the following series of harmonic roots: A lydian, I-II-VI-VII-III-I.

5. Harmonize a descending major scale with major triads exclusively.

6. Harmonize the ascending Enigmatic scale with major and minor triads.

7. Harmonize the following melody with chords by thirds.

Ex. 3-49

8. Extend the following passage for two clarinets and two bassoons.

Ex. 3-50

9. Using C as a tonal center (but no prevailing scale), create a quiet mood in the string orchestra while triads progress in chromatic relationships of the second and third. End on a six-three tonic equivalent.

10. Write a succession of staccato chords in the brasses. Establish several tritone root movements.

11. Construct a sequence of major seventh chords and build a string quartet passage on the sequential idea.

12. Harmonize the following melody in four string parts using dominant seventh chords exclusively. Much contrary and oblique motion and several inversions should be used.

Ex. 3-51

13. Write a series of sequences including seventh and ninth chords.

14. Include several kinds of seventh and ninth chords in an organ interlude.

15. In a short section for piano dominated by ninth chords, use loud and rough fourth inversions.

16. Expand this piano passage of eleventh and thirteenth chords preserving the general character.

Ex. 3-52

17. In string music of sustained chords by thirds include several eleventh and thirteenth chords.

18. Write a short triadic piece for one piano, four hands, in which sudden fifteenth formations interrupt the mood.

19. Write a lyric line for solo trumpet with a quiet divisi string background of twelve-note chords.

20. Construct twelve-note chords for full band that punctuate a rapid solo timpani passage.

Chords by Fourths

TWENTIETH-CENTURY composers use quartal harmony (chords by fourths) as well as the tertian harmony (chords by thirds) of Classic and Romantic practice. Quartal materials stem from ornamentation of the triad (*a*) and from the techniques of medieval polyphony (*b*).

Ex. 4-1

Chords by fourths are built by superimposing intervals of the fourth. In other spacings, most of the chord members must be placed a fourth apart in order to preserve the distinctive quartal sound; otherwise the quartal structures may sound like eleventh, thirteenth, or added-note chords.

Ex. 4-2

by 4ths   by 4ths   11th   13th   added-note

Three-, four-, and five-note chords by perfect fourths have a pentatonic flavor. The five-note form contains all the steps of the diatonic pentatonic scale.

Ex. 4-3

Chords by perfect fourths are ambiguous in that, like all chords built by equidistant intervals (diminished seventh chords or augmented triads), any member can function as the root. The indifference of this rootless harmony to tonality places the burden of key verification upon the voice with the most active melodic line.

Ex. 4-4

THREE-NOTE CHORDS BY FOURTHS

Three kinds of intervallic arrangement of three-note chords by fourths are possible: perfect-perfect, perfect-augmented, and augmented-perfect. The augmented-augmented arrangement is impracticable because the first and third notes are enharmonically identical.

Ex. 4-5

In all types of three-note chords by fourths two inversions are possible. Inverting chords having two perfect fourths helps prevent the harmonic monotony of uniform intervals. Either inversion can be used as a fundamental structure because of the presence of the strong perfect fifth. If the resonant interval of the perfect fifth is allowed to dominate the texture, the second—created by the inverted seventh—often sounds like a note added to a simple chordal formation. Positions featuring the perfect fifth give quartal harmony variety of color.

Ex. 4-6

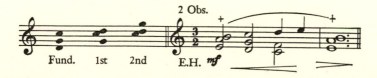

The variety presented by open spacing increases harmonic expressiveness:

Ex. 4-7

2 Tpts. (sord.)

Any note in a perfect quartal chord may be doubled as well as any other note. Doubling of the outer parts enriches harmonic color and doubling of inner parts strengthens any moving voice.

Ex. 4-8

A succession of chords by perfect fourths does not fall within the intervallic make-up of any one scale. If the chords are to be made to fit a scale pattern, miscellaneous fourths must be used (*a*). Chords by perfect fourths, therefore, are chromatically more supple than chords with perfect and augmented fourths. The scale tones used as building roots for perfect-fourth chords will be duplicated at different tonal levels, indicating a polytonal potential(*b*).

Ex. 4-9

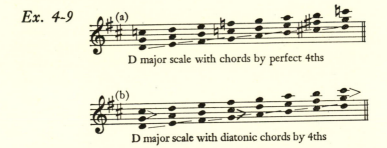

D major scale with chords by perfect 4ths

D major scale with diatonic chords by 4ths

The perfect-perfect chord is seldom used as a dissonant structure. The absence of a sharp interval, the equality of the perfect fourths, and the mildness of the minor seventh create a texture that is consonant in a quartal context. Any member of this chord is free to skip.

Ex. 4-10

In chords containing an augmented fourth (perfect-augmented or augmented-perfect) the upper note of the tritone resolves best to the nearest note of the prevailing melodic or scale formation. If the neighboring tones of the scale lie equal distances away, either direction is taken.

Ex. 4-11

Any chord tone in any type of three- or four-note quartal chord may skip a fourth or seventh if the other tones remain stationary. The result is a larger (four- or five-note) version of the same chord.

Ex. 4-12

Any type of three-note chord by fourths can progress diatonically, chromatically, or by a skip to any other chord by fourths if one voice moves with strong melodic purpose.

Ex. 4-13

Clarity is difficult to achieve with chords by fourths in low registers; they tend to flow more easily in upper voices—woodwinds or women's voices. A pedal point lessens any dissonant tone's need for resolution.

Ex. 4-14

When a florid voice is added to three-note chords by fourths greater harmonic freedom is possible.

Ex. 4-15

Chords by fourths may be approached or left by triads when the uppermost note is prepared,

Ex. 4-16

when suspensions are not resolved,

Ex. 4-17

and when the sixth or ninth is added to a cadential tertian tonic.

Ex. 4-18

When both tertian and quartal chords appear in a progression, it is advisable to employ devices in the tertian harmony that bring out the flavor of the perfect fourth. Chords by fourths may be approached or left by ninth chords when the fourth inversion of the ninth chord is used with the root in the top voice (the prominent seventh, spanning two fourths, acts as a binder for the two chordal categories);

Ex. 4-19

by seventh chords when the third and fifth of parallel seventh chords are replaced by the fourth;

Ex. 4-20

and by thirteenth chords when they are arranged so that fourths predominate.

Ex. 4-21

In quartal cadences the final chord is more powerful in its inverted form.

Ex. 4-22

Quartal chord members move so freely that in cadences made solely of chords by fourths the next to the last fourth chord may have any bass tone.

Ex. 4-23

Chords by fourths are used as "dominants" in cadences of any harmonic idiom. Any mixture of chords may be used in quartal cadences if the interval of the fourth is predominant in the harmony.

FOUR-NOTE CHORDS BY FOURTHS

A quartal structure more resonant than a three-note chord by fourths is made by adding another fourth to the chord. The new tone forms a consonant interval (tenth) with the bass tone and adds color and variety to quartal harmony. Four-note chords by fourths are extremely useful in their three inverted forms because of the variety of intervals they contain.

Ex. 4-24

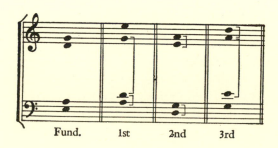

Fund.   1st   2nd   3rd

Moving through inversions of the same chord will produce real harmonic movement without a root change.

Ex. 4-25

Four-note chords resolve easily to chords by thirds when two voices move conjunctly while the others remain stationary. Three-note quartal chords with a doubling are useful in this context.

Ex. 4-26

When the augmented fourth is present in a four-note chord by fourths the tritone moves easily if placed at the top of the chord.

Ex. 4-27

Compound construction (thirds and fourths) brings fresh color to quartal harmony. A third may be added above or below a three-note chord by fourths. If the added third is major the chord sounds consonant; if the third is minor the chord sounds less consonant.

Ex. 4-28

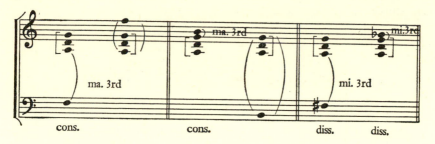

The compound three-note quartal chord with the major third added is effective when used as a cadential tonic. When used as passing chords both types (major or minor thirds) are equally useful. A third above and below the quartal structure may appear with it simultaneously as a five-note chord; this formation is lush in sound and functions particularly well in progressions containing tertian or polychordal structures.

Ex. 4-29

The chromatic introduction of a chord by fourths may cause a sudden shift of tonality or scale formation.

Ex. 4-30

Chords by fourths may be arranged in fifths as easily as chords by thirds are arranged in sixths.

Ex. 4-31

When fifths dominate a quartal chord the fourths become restless. It is advisable to resolve the fourth to a third of a compound quartal chord before returning to the pure chord by fourths.

MULTI-NOTE CHORDS BY FOURTHS

Chords built of superimposed perfect fourths are consonant to and include the five-note chord. The six-note chord results in a categorical change in tension because of the sharp dissonant interval. These six- (or more) note chords belong to the dissonant group of three-, four-, and five-note chords containing an augmented fourth. It is good to exploit the relationship of a dissonant group with a consonant group.

Ex. 4-32

Thirteenth chords and multi-note quartal chords often contain the same notes. The similarity is theoretical, not aural. If thirds overrun a six- or seven-note chord, the ear hears a thirteenth formation. If a six- or seven-note chord is overrun by fourths, a chord by fourths sounds.

Ex. 4-33

13th   chord by 4ths

If the number of thirds and fourths is equal the chord may be used as a pivotal structure and regarded as belonging to either the tertian or quartal category, or to both.

Twelve different notes may be placed a perfect fourth apart before one is repeated (twelve-note chords by fourths).

Ex. 4-34

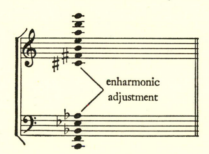

enharmonic
adjustment

As the number of chord members increases, the linear potential decreases. A touch of parallel movement, an interrupting unison, or a suddenly enriched dominant will prevent harmonic suffocation. If muddy sounds are not wanted, place the larger intervals at the bottom of the chord and omit a member. Voices may be clustered and the distinctive quality of quartal harmony preserved by the isolation of orchestral timbre:

Ex. 4-35

Source Material

Quartal harmony:

Alban Berg, Wozzeck (red.), p. 45 (Universal)
Leonard Bernstein, Seven Anniversaries for Piano, p. 3 (Witmark)
Valentino Bucchi, Piano Sonatina (1938), p. 3 (Zerboni)
Aaron Copland, Piano Fantasy, p. 2 (Boosey)
Paul Hindemith, Nobilissima Visione (orchestral suite), p. 49 (Schott)
Arthur Honegger, King David (red.), p. 5 (Foetisch)
Arnold Schoenberg, Kammersymphonie Op. 9, p. 1 (Universal)
Roger Sessions, Symphony No. 2, p. 67 (G. Schirmer)
Igor Stravinsky, Septet, p. 11 (Boosey)
William Walton, Concerto for Viola and Orchestra (red.), p. 12 (Oxford)
Anton Webern, Piano Variations Op. 27, pp. 5–6 (Universal)

Applications

1. Write sequential passages for flute, oboe, and clarinet. Use chords by perfect fourths exclusively.

2. Write a short presto for two trumpets and trombone. Feature perfect-augmented and augmented-perfect chords by fourths.

3. Write an example of three-part quartal harmony for two violins and viola over a cello pedal point. Ornament the pedal.

4. Continue the following passage for trumpets preserving the general character.

Ex. 4-36

5. Compose an original piece for women's voices (SSA) featuring chords by fourths. Other textures may be included. Use the following text, Psalm 107: "They mount up to the heaven, they go down again to the depths: their soul is melted because of trouble."

6. Continue the following idea for piano.

Ex. 4-37

7. Add soprano, alto, and tenor voices; use chords by fourths.

Ex. 4-38

(bass voice)

8. Harmonize the following melody for woodwind quartet allowing quartal harmony to dominate the passage.

Ex. 4-39

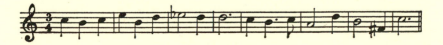

9. Write several melodies and harmonize them with a predominantly quartal texture. Any medium and any number of parts may be used.

10. Extend the following string-quartet opening. Feature pentatonic melodic and quartal harmonic writing.

Ex. 4-40

| # Added-Note Chords

AN ADDED-NOTE chord is a basic harmonic formation whose textural quality has been modified by the imposition of tones not found in the original chord. The tones to be added form one or more major or minor seconds with any member of a chord by thirds or by fourths. These added notes are usually placed a second above or below any member to avoid creating seventh, ninth, compound chords, etc. The added tone or tones are modifying elements attached to a chord of clear directional powers and, as color modifications, change the texture rather than the function of the basic structure. Traditional examples of added-note chords are to be found in the cadential tonic six-five and the French augmented sixth chord.

AUGMENTED SIXTH CHORDS

The augmented sixth is a likely chord to add notes to because its directional pull is sufficiently strong to be unimpaired by the addition of color tones. The French augmented sixth is a prime example; here a major second is added above the middle tone of the basic Italian augmented sixth chord. This attached note alters neither the function nor the formal meaning of the Italian chord but creates fringe color (the augmented sixth interval gives the Italian chord its motivating power and the interval a third from the bottom gives it its fundamental flavor).

Twentieth-century added-note technique employs five basic augmented sixth chords to which seconds may be attached. These chords consist of the interval of the augmented sixth with: a major third (Italian); a minor third; an augmented octave with a major third; a doubly augmented octave with a major third; and an augmented third.

Ex. 5-1

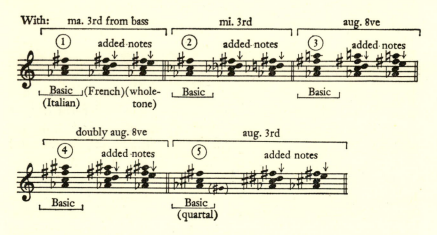

The formation with the minor third is a color variant of the Italian augmented sixth with the major third. The basic augmented sixth chords with the augmented octave and with the doubly augmented octave are ninth textures and are useful in passages featuring ninth, eleventh, and thirteenth chords. The augmented sixth chord with the augmented third is useful in a quartal context and is often spelled enharmonically. In any chord containing the interval of the augmented sixth the voices spanning the interval have a tendency to expand, descend chromatically, or move obliquely (one voice held).

Ex. 5-2

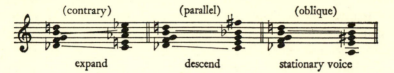

Several major and minor seconds may be added simultaneously to any form of the augmented sixth chord without changing its function. The chord has a strong tendency to move onward regardless of the number of notes attached to it.

Ex. 5-3

Augmented sixth chords with two or more added notes resolve most naturally to added-note chords of another variety, because of their common secundal texture.

OTHER ADDED-NOTE CHORDS

Major and minor seconds may be added not only to augmented sixth formations but to most chords by thirds and fourths. Added notes are not ornamental tones sounding with a chord but true color members that rival the third in color potential. They add spice and increase the harmonic density.

Ex. 5-4

Major and minor seconds may be added above or below any member of a major or minor triad but the lower the added note is placed in the chord the less resonant the formation.

Ex. 5-5

Adding a note above a major third diffuses the color of this rich member. The minor third is somewhat less affected by an added note.

The diminished triad will always be a sharp-textured chord regardless of what added note is applied or where it is added. In the augmented triad with major seconds added above or below any member, the texture is still whole-tone; the minor-second additions are more useful because they make possible intervallic variety. Additions to seventh and ninth chords are more frequently minor seconds because a major-second addition sometimes results in duplication of a chord member.

Ex. 5-6

*In some cases, a triad or seventh chord with an added note may
resemble a ninth chord. A look at the context can determine the
true identity of the chord.*

In some cases, a triad or seventh chord with an added note may
resemble a ninth chord. A look at the context can determine the
true identity of the chord.

In an added-note seventh or ninth chord even the sharply dissonant added tones do not compete with the seventh or ninth for
dissonant-tone movement attention; the added tones are not strong
contenders for resolution. They cling to inverted as well as to
fundamental chords and may be doubled at will. Doubling the
added note in outer voices is effective when it occurs as successive
octaves in melodic coupling. Over-all coupling sounds well when
used in an entire body of added-note harmony.

Ex. 5-7

Seconds are added to chords by perfect fourths in the following
order for sonority: for mild texture, the major second below the
seventh, above the fourth, below the fourth, and above the "root";
and for sharp texture, the minor second above the seventh, below
the seventh, above the fourth, below the fourth, and above the
"root." The lower the second is placed in the chord the less resonant the formation:

Ex. 5-8

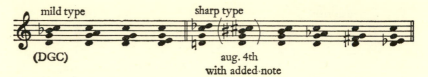

It is possible to regard the above chords either as triads with added notes or as incomplete seventh and ninth chords with added notes. The chords will sound like added-note chords by fourths if they appear in a passage dominated by fourth chords and like added-note chords by thirds if a preponderance of chords by thirds is used.

The chromatic-second addition to chords by perfect fourths creates a sharp texture which blends well with the texture of augmented fourth chords without added notes. Whether the seconds fastened to augmented-fourth chord members are major or minor, the chord will always be of sharp texture because of the major seventh interval in the basic formation.

Ex. 5-9

Augmented fourth chords with and without added notes sound well side by side because they both belong to the category of sharp textures.

Ex. 5-10

In any kind of added-note chord two general textures are possible, a mild type having no sharp dissonance and a sharp type having at least one sharp dissonance.

Ex. 5-11

Added-note chords of the mild type often stop harmonic flow by their tendency to form a cadence, and when used extensively cause harmonic progressions to become paralyzed. A flow can be maintained by mixing freely the mild and sharp types.

The progressive motion of added-note chords is governed by the basic harmony to which added notes are attached. Such devices as cadences, sequences, and traditional harmonic formulas help protect the basic chords from the debilitating effect of crowding seconds.

Ex. 5-12

Added-note chords are effective as such only when a clear and definite harmonic progression is implied by the basic chords or is previously established by chords without added notes. This is particularly true of those chords that contain many notes spread over a wide range. Notes may be attached to complex basic chords if the structures are first clearly stated without the color tones. If notes are added to a complex basic chord without textural preparation, a chord of a larger basic formation—not of added notes —is heard. A large compound chord and a complex added-note chord are often identical. Unless a firm harmonic progression is felt under the complex added-note structure, a compound harmonic texture will prevail.

Added-note chords are often secundal in appearance; an added-note chord and a chord by seconds are sometimes identical. It is only within the general context of a section of music that a difference can be seen.

Occasionally, added notes are placed outside the original octave range. This wider spacing produces greater freedom of harmonic movement and clearer focusing of the dissonant added tones.

Ex. 5-13

A special category of this type of chord with its added note outside the octave is that of the triad in close position with a note added below. A triad (major, minor, diminished, or augmented) is placed in the upper voices and a major or minor second above or below any of the members is added as the bottom voice, often in octaves for balance. A wide variety of chordal structures is possible; there are thirty-six such chords.

Ex. 5-14

Although some of these structures resemble traditional chords by thirds they do not function as such in a context of added-note harmony.

Progression in this type of added-note harmony is often governed by an upper melodic line. Each note of a melody, except ornamental tones, may be considered a member of a major, minor, diminished, or augmented triad. A bass line is then constructed from notes a second from any triadic member (Ex. 5-14). Bass notes for the bottom line are chosen to form the kind of outer-voice relationship that best suits the desired texture and phrase shapes:

Ex. 5-15

This type of added-note chord is most effective when used in harmonic progressions consisting solely of the same type of added-note structures. Primary and secondary relationships are not relevant, melody being the governing factor. Textural consistency is insured by chordal spacing, and freedom of linear movement is made possible by the wide selection of bass notes.

Source Material

Added-note harmony:

Paul Ben-Haim, 5 Pieces for Piano Op. 34, p. 10 (Negen)
Benjamin Britten, The Turn of the Screw (red.), pp. 41–44 (Boosey)
Carlos Chávez, Sonatina for Piano, p. 1 (Cos Cob)
Aaron Copland, Billy the Kid (ballet suite), p. 85 (Boosey)
Luigi Dallapiccola, Volo di Notte (red.), p. 37 (Universal)
Alberto Ginastera, Piano Sonata, p. 24 (Barry)
M. Camargo Guarnieri, Den-Báu, p. 3 (Music Press)
Paul Hindemith, Das Marienleben, p. 69 (Schott)
Arthur Honegger, Jeanne d'Arc au Bûcher (red.), pp. 20–21 (Salabert)
Charles Ives, Violin Sonata No. 4, pp. 4–5 (Arrow)
André Jolivet, Bassoon Concerto (red.), p. 32 (Heugel)
Riccardo Malipiero, Sonata for Violin and Piano, p. 3 (Zerboni)
Frank Martin, Piano Prelude No. 4 (Universal)
Peter Mennin, The Christmas Story (red.), p. 26 (C. Fischer)
Gian Carlo Menotti, Sebastian Suite, p. 11 (Ricordi)
Darius Milhaud, Christophe Colomb (red.), p. 8 (Universal)
Igor Stravinsky, Fire-Bird Suite, p. 77 (Kalmus)
Antonio Veretti, Piano Sonatina, p. 9 (Ricordi)

Applications

1. Construct a segment of music for chamber orchestra featuring various types of augmented sixth chords.

2. Modulate by means of various kinds of augmented sixth chords through several keys. Score the example for two pianos.

3. Write a short triadic passage for woodwinds that is interrupted by a solo horn introducing an added-note variant of the initial material, in strings.

4. Write added-note chords for piano, right hand, over this left hand ground bass. Extend to sixteen measures.

Ex. 5-16

5. Harmonize a folk tune with added-note chords of the mild type. Score for voice and piano.

6. Write an allegro section for brasses and feature added-note chords of the sharp variety.

7. Write a sarcastically rhythmic passage for string quartet. Feature augmented fourth chords with added notes.

8. Write an example of coupled added-note chords for band.

9. Extend the following piano idea, preserving the general character.

Ex. 5-17

10. Write an orchestral crescendo in which the harmonic volume increases. Start with small added-note formations and finish with a cadence of complex added-note structures.

11. Harmonize the following melody for strings with triads in the violins and violas, and the added notes in the cellos and basses (in octaves).

Ex. 5-18

| # Chords by Seconds

THERE ARE THREE categories of intervallic materials from which chords may be built: thirds or sixths (tertian), fourths or fifths (quartal), and seconds or sevenths (secundal). The addition of seconds to chords by thirds or fourths, or the filling-in of the mixed intervals of compound chords for coloristic purposes, does not produce chords by seconds; these are added-note chords. But out of context such chords may be called by either name.

THREE-NOTE CHORDS BY SECONDS

Both major and minor seconds may be used in the construction of chords by seconds (the augmented second is tertian in effect). There are four intervallic types of three-note chords by seconds: major-major, major-minor, minor-major, and minor-minor. Arranged in an order of consonance progressing to dissonance they are:

Ex. 6-1

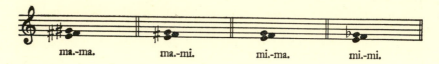

Two inversions of each are possible.

Ex. 6-2

Chords by seconds may be arranged in sevenths, as chords by thirds may be arranged in sixths and chords by fourths in fifths.

Ex. 6-3

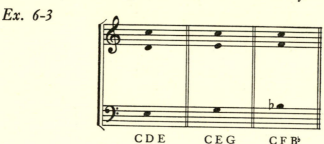

When chords by seconds are used in close position they cramp easily and become percussive in the low register. Spacing in intervals of the seventh and ninth gives the muscle-bound chords by seconds linear freedom and room for activity of the parts.

Ex. 6-4

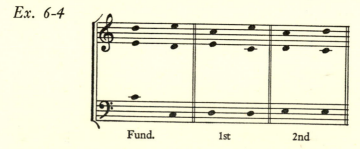

In the preceding example, spacing produces chords similar to ninths, but in a secundal context they are chords by seconds in open position.

In major, minor, or the five other modal scales, only the first three types of three-note chords are found naturally; the minor-minor is derived from chromatic or synthetic scales.

Ex. 6-5

For solidarity, the bass note of secundal harmony, whether root, second, or third, is doubled (*a*). For mildness of texture the most consonant note over the bass is doubled regardless of whether or not it is the root (*b*). For sharpness of texture the most dissonant note over the bass is doubled (*c*).

Ex. 6-6

A dissonant tone is a restless tone that often asks for resolution. In fundamental position and in second inversion of secundal harmony of any intervallic type the dissonant tone is the second of the chord. In the first inversion it is the third of the chord, except in the minor-major first inversion, where the root is most dissonant.

Ex. 6-7

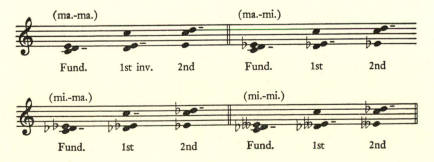

In the first inversion of the major-major the root becomes the dissonant tone if it lies below the third.

Ex. 6-8

1st inv.

If the dissonant tone is a member of a sharp dissonant interval (major seventh or minor second), one of the members that forms the sharp interval is, for smoothness of line, best approached and left conjunctly or by repetition. If the dissonant tone is not a member of a sharp dissonant interval, it is approached and left freely.

Ex. 6-9

Three-note secundal harmony has a unique flavor.

Ex. 6-10

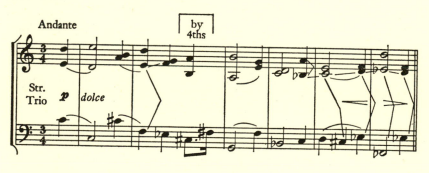

MULTI-NOTE CHORDS BY SECONDS

Four- and five-note chords by seconds move contrapuntally with difficulty. Linear motion can be obtained by including in the progression three-note chords by seconds or chords by fourths. The sevenths (inverted seconds) that are present in chords by fourths blend with the seconds in chords by seconds and leave space for movement of the parts.

Ex. 6-11

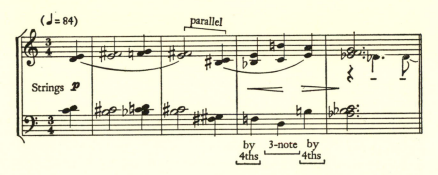

In the preceding example chords by seconds are used at the phrase breath without disturbing the parallel position of the parts.

A single chord by seconds can be enlarged to encompass an entire scale, diatonic, chromatic, or original. It may or may not be a cluster depending upon the type of harmony that surrounds it. This thickened harmony is best combined with polychordal or compound harmony before it hardens:

Ex. 6-12

Source Material

Secundal harmony:

Béla Bartók, String Quartet No. 3, p. 3 (Boosey)
Karl-Birger Blomdahl, Aniara (red.), p. 105 (Schott)
Aaron Copland, Piano Sonata, p. 14 (Boosey)
Claude Debussy, Préludes Vol. II, p. 73 (Durand)
Darius Milhaud, Christophe Colomb (red.), p. 143 (Universal)
Francis Poulenc, Promenades for Piano, p. 13 (Chester)
Carl Ruggles, Men and Mountains, p. 12 (New Music)
Camillo Togni, Fantasia Concertante (flute and strings), pp. 4–5 (Zerboni)
Heitor Villa-Lobos, String Quartet No. 3, p. 32 (Eschig)

CLUSTERS

When a passage is dominated by chords by seconds and arranged in predominantly uninverted forms so that most of the voices are a second apart, the chords are called clusters. These are not true chords by seconds, in part because of their generally consistent spacing but mainly because of the lack of defined inner voice movement. When large clusters are used, handling the voices is accomplished solely by considering the two-part contrapuntal frame formed by the outer voices. The seconds fill in this frame while expanding and contracting the clusters to form good outer-part writing.

Ex. 6-13

Most scale formations or their parts may be clustered. The chromatic scale is the least useful because when clustered it becomes tiresome quickly. A seven-note scale may be clustered modally in seven different ways; and a two-octave scale, in fourteen.

Ex. 6-14

Changing, in progression, the intervallic make-up and number of chord members gives cluster harmony textural interest and momentum.

Ex. 6-15

Subtleties of cluster part-writing are difficult to compose or notate for the piano. Chamber combinations and the orchestra can more fully utilize clusters and better accommodate notation. Chromatic clusters are often notated for keyboard instruments with one note written so that it runs through the entire cluster, the cluster to be played with palms or arms.

Ex. 6-16

A chromatic cluster can be scored for instruments in such a way that the cluster is broken into chordal units.

Ex. 6-17

When clusters move in parallel motion the progression is purely melodic. Changing the parallel motion to similar motion in some of the voices adds textural interest, and using occasional octaves in the two outer parts accentuates the color.

Clusters progress harmonically by expanding and contracting, changing the intervallic construction, omitting chord members, and shifting voice colors. Large clusters are powerful in dramatic punctuations but smaller clusters are more agile and generally easier to handle.

The consonant-dissonant quality of cluster harmony may oppose or parallel the quality of the counterpoint of the outer voices. Consonant or dissonant clusters (diatonic or chromatic) may be used in all possible combinations with consonant or dissonant outer voices.

Clusters may be formed from one complete scale of any type or from two or more contrasting scales.

Ex. 6-18

A cluster is not always introduced by sounding all its tones simultaneously. When the tones of a cluster are sounded consecutively they are effective if each note is held until the last enters. These arpeggio versions of the cluster contribute variety to secundal patterns. They may unfold from top to bottom, bottom to top, or from the center to the extremities.

Ex. 6-19

The consonant or dissonant aspect of a cluster's character may be accentuated by the way in which its members enter. Or accentuation may be determined by sounding consonant or dissonant intervals of the cluster beforehand:

Ex. 6-20

Large clusters may accumulate through the additive use of chords by thirds or fourths, polychords, or smaller clusters.

Ex. 6-21

Two or more clusters, derived from one scale or different scales, may be used simultaneously as a polycluster. The roots of the various cluster units of a polycluster may form a chord by seconds (*a*), a triad (*b*), or a chord by fourths (*c*).

Ex. 6-22

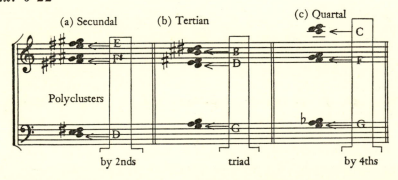

Space must be left between the cluster units to allow them to sound distinctly. The larger each cluster, the wider must be the space.

The number of contrapuntal voices involved in polycluster harmony is automatically doubled if the cluster sizes fluctuate. Each cluster is then outlined by two independent voices.

Ex. 6-23

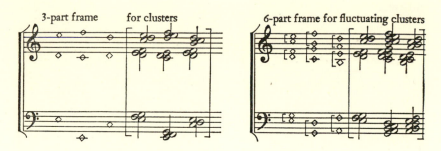

Varying the outer voices by contrary, oblique, or parallel movement will produce clusters of changing sizes. As clusters increase in size, harmonic tension increases; as clusters decrease in
size, instrumental color can become concentrated because of overlapped and doubled voices.

Clusters may be broken (arpeggios by seconds) but will sound
like clusters only if cluster harmony has been previously established. They will sound like scales if the broken clusters are not
clearly part of a cluster context.

Ex. 6-24

Ornamental tones increase harmonic circulation in passages of clusters.

Ex. 6-25

Translating traditional harmony into cluster harmony by arbitrarily filling in the space is calculative and usually without musical impetus. Clusters more effectively stem from the secundal harmony that generates them because of the common interval of the second. Clusters are used with chords by seconds, but occasionally in conjunction with or in contrast to other types of harmony. When clusters or chords by seconds are used with chords by thirds or fourths they can take part in progressions of functional root relationships.

Ex. 6-26

Source Material

Clusters:

Alban Berg, Wozzeck (red.), p. 33 (Universal)
Ernest Bloch, Piano Sonata, p. 1 (Carisch)
Henry Cowell, Silt of the Reel (Universal)
Alan Hovhaness, Magnificat, p. 26 (Peters)
Charles Ives, 19 Songs (Majority) (New Music)
Wallingford Riegger, Music for Brass Choir, p. 1 (Merrymount)
Edgard Varèse, Ionisation, p. 21 (New Music)

Applications

1. Harmonize the following melody for string trio using chords by seconds.

Ex. 6-27

2. Write a three-part Elegy for two clarinets and bass clarinet featuring chords by seconds.

3. Write a short Presto for three muted trumpets featuring minor-minor chords by seconds.

4. Write a four-part Prelude for string quartet employing three-note chords by seconds (with doubling), four-note chords by seconds, and chords by fourths (with the inverted seventh).

5. Write a Capriccio for two pianos in which diatonic, pentatonic, and chromatic clusters are used.

6. Write a slow passage for string orchestra allowing clusters to expand and contract.

7. Write an example of orchestral music which includes several polyclusters.

CHAPTER
SEVEN | Polychords

A POLYCHORD IS the simultaneous combination of two or more chords from different harmonic areas. The segments of the polychord are referred to as chordal units. The beginnings of polychords may be traced to double and triple pedal point, where hints of bitonality, caused by the relationship of the passing chords to the pedal chord, lie in the passing harmony.

Ex. 7-1

Polyharmony is seldom polytonal. Polytonality is present only when the chordal units that make up the structure adhere to separate keys.

Ex. 7-2

Polytonal type

Polychords that are not polytonal are considerably more flexible and versatile; the harmonic areas of both chordal units shift often.

Ex. 7-3

Clear grouping of the chordal units is a requisite of polyharmony, and rearranging the tones of these units can destroy the polychordal organization.

Ex. 7-4

(not a polychord)

TWO TRIADIC UNITS

Overtones resulting from a fundamental tone and from those overtones themselves may produce polyharmony:

Ex. 7-5

The resonance of a polychord is determined by the intervallic structure of the bottom chordal unit and the power of its separate tones to generate overtones. The second inversion of the major triad as a bottom unit is the most resonant chordal unit upon which polyharmony can be erected, because its internal spacing is closest to that of the harmonic series; the major third of the fundamental triad in close position is not as close to the size of the perfect fifth of the overtone series as is the perfect fourth of the six-four chord. When the tones of the bottom triad are spread apart, the fundamental position is most sonorous. Any position or inversion of the upper triad may be used depending upon the kind of outer-voice relationship desired.

The upper triad of a polychord depends upon its proximity to the overtones of the third and fifth of the lower triad for resonance. A complete inventory of major-major polychords may be made by building the upper major triads on the notes of a cycle of perfect fifths that begins with the bass note of the bottom six-four chordal unit. The triads are added, in turn, to the bottom six-four chord, creating a rising order, based upon the cycle of fifths, which places the chords in a natural sequence of decreasing consonance and increasing dissonance. The last six polychords are noticeably less resonant; the sound of number 11 is almost a dull thud.

Ex. 7-6

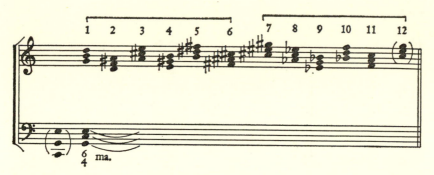

The density of the polychordal structure is determined by spac-ing. Placing chordal units well apart allows for maximum tonal vibration. Contrasting instrumentation of the chordal units clearly defines the contrasting harmonic zones. Doubling the consonant intervals gives strength. A tone common to the units helps blend the component parts.

The relationship of the bottom and top tones of the polychord is important. Consonant outer-voice resonance spreads its effective-ness throughout the formation and dissonant outer voices do the same.

Ex. 7-7

A polychord gains resonance if smaller intervals are placed in the upper register and wider intervals are placed in the lower register. A polychord like number 7 (Ex. 7-6) becomes less nebulous by careful spacing.

Ex. 7-8

Although close spacing and monochrome scoring produce cloudiness, the result is a valuable addition to the over-all fluctuating tension of harmony.

Ex. 7-9

The closer the dissonant tones are placed to each other, the higher the degree of tension; but unless clearly defined as part of a chordal unit, the different harmonic areas will run into each other and polyharmony cease to exist.

Ex. 7-10

Nevertheless, this added-note chord can be projected polychord-ally by strongly contrasted instrumentation (C major woodwinds and F♯ major strings).

If the upper unit in a polychord forms a chord by thirds with the bottom unit (numbers 1 and 12, Ex. 7-6), the ear identifies such a structure, out of context, as a non-polychord. But the chord may be unmistakably part of the polychordal category by reason of context when surrounded by polyharmony.

Ex. 7-11

When the lowest note of the polychord is placed somewhere below the bass clef low F, the harmony becomes muddy unless an open-position chord is used. (The "muddy" polychord is nevertheless a valuable structure under appropriate dramatic con-ditions.)

Ex. 7-12

As a polychord is transposed upward it loses body and resonance but gains brilliance (*a*). Drastic complexion changes occur in lower register transpositions (*b*):

Ex. 7-13

A polychord may be made up of any kind of triads. When it is constructed of major triads it is most consonant and resonant, becoming progressively less so as minor, then augmented, and finally diminished triads are included. The qualities of the twelve major-minor (named from the bottom upward) possibilities may be observed when the upper units are added to the bottom chord in a rising cycle of fifths beginning with the bass note of the bottom unit. Numbers 4, 5, 6, 9, and 12 are more useful because of their resonant character.

Ex. 7-14

A minor over a major triad is richer than a major over a minor; the upper triad in the first formation receives additional support from tones of the lower chord other than the bottom tone from which it is generated.

Ex. 7-15

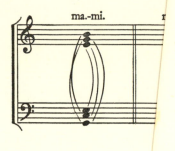

All polychords
triad are identif
the chromati

Ex. 7-18

Of the minor-major polychc
use because they are more res

Ex. 7-16

In minor-minor polychords, the resonant numbers 1, 5, and 9 are most frequently used.

Ex. 7-17

...containing at least one diminished or augmented ...ed as chromatic polychords. The most supple of ...s are:

When the bottom chordal unit is augmented or diminished it is advisable to spread the voices of the lower triad to avoid lower-register crowding. The most resonant polychords in this category are:

Ex. 7-19

The direction of polyharmony is determined by linear movement. The counterpoint of chords (counterchords) is derived from a two-part linear frame of single-tone lines. Two kinds of counterchordal techniques serve as a working basis for polyharmonic writing: two-part counterpoint used as the outer voices of polyharmony,

Ex. 7-20

and two-part counterpoint used as the roots of triads of both units making up the polyharmony. The notes of the basic two-part framework of roots move freely between inner and outer voices:

Ex. 7-21

Any note of any melodic line can become the root, third, or fifth of a major, minor, diminished, or augmented triad. Whether the composer works from the upper or lower triad, the great number of combinations of triads that are possible gives him a wide choice of textures within which the harmonic tension can fluctuate.

Ex. 7-22

Polyharmonic progressions touch so many key areas that tonality cannot be secured through the harmonic personality of a prevailing scale. Tonality is established by the tonal implications of a predominating melodic line or by harmonic gravitation to a dominating chord. Resonant polychords play the tonic role most convincingly; a wealth of invention must be saved for the cadence if a firm tonal center is desired. A tonality may be formed by the melody,

Ex. 7-23

or from a characteristic chord.

Ex. 7-24

Prolonged passages of pure polychords can result in tiring mass resonance; the richness and thickness stifle inner voices. Modification of the lines by ornamentation freshens the texture since attention is captured by individual voice activity:

Ex. 7-25

Unison and two-voice interruptions revitalize the polychordal texture.

Ex. 7-26

Omission of notes of either chordal unit lightens the texture and contributes harmonic flexibility.

Ex. 7-27

When polychords are used as architectural harmonic pillars, their dynamic contrast with other types of harmony is refreshing.

Ex. 7-28

Source Material

Polychords, two triadic units:

Béla Bartók, String Quartet No. 5, p. 87 (Boosey)
Peter Racine Fricker, Piano Concerto Op. 19 (red.), p. 40 (Schott)
Roy Harris, Soliloquy and Dance, for viola and piano, p. 7 (G. Schirmer)
Charles Ives, Piano Sonata No. 2, p. 65 (Arrow)
Arthur Honegger, Symphony No. 5, p. 1 (Salabert)
Albert Roussel, Bacchus et Ariane, p. 57 (Durand)
William Schuman, Symphony for Strings, p. 8 (G. Schirmer)
Igor Stravinsky, The Rake's Progress (red.), p. 195 (Boosey)

THREE OR MORE TRIADIC UNITS

Chordal units in polyharmony are often built upon different overtones of the same series. There are four kinds of polychords with three or more units: those whose upper units are built on the third and fifth of the bottom triad (rarely the root);

Ex. 7-29

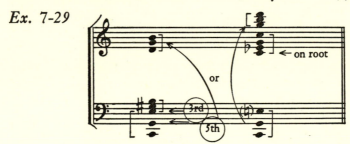

those whose upper units are built on overtones (at any octave level) of the third and fifth of the bottom triad;

Ex. 7-30

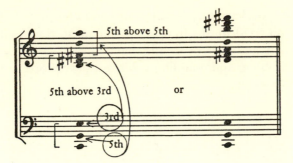

those whose upper units are built on overtones of the overtones of the third and fifth of the bottom triad;

Ex. 7-31

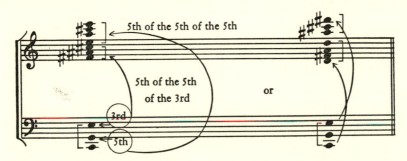

and those whose upper notes are built on overtones of the root, third, or fifth of triads other than the bottom triad.

Ex. 7-32

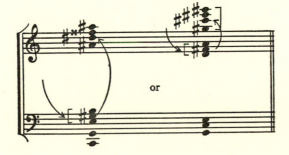

Multi-unit polyharmony is so massive and complex that the notes of the bottom triad must often be spread apart. Some units should be overlapped and others should have the space between them widened. Doubling and coupling enlarge a polychord without adding to its complexity.

Ex. 7-33

Overlapping in a three-unit chord may result in a two-unit chord.

Ex. 7-34

Multi-unit polychords (usually not polytonal) are used for brief periods of time. Their natural habitat is a climactic section,

Ex. 7-35

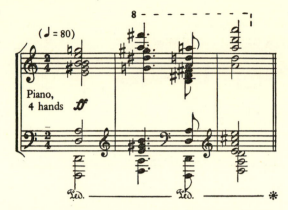

or a fast but quiet section.

Ex. 7-36

NON-TRIADIC UNITS

Polychords consisting of seventh chord units are seldom used in extended passages but more often in brief chordal groups that intensify a single line or a two-part statement,

Ex. 7-37

or as a sforzando chord.

Ex. 7-38

Some polychords whose individual units are seventh chords contain one or more notes in common, which makes for a homogeneous sound;

Ex. 7-39

and some have no notes in common.

Ex. 7-40

When chords other than chords by thirds are used as building units in polychords, textural clarity becomes more of a problem. Polychordal formations of chords by fourths are, in effect, enlarged versions of three-note chords by fourths. And if all the units are secundal, a polycluster results. However, quartal and secundal units are used with those by thirds in a polychord of mixed chordal units. Chords by seconds function sonorously as the uppermost unit of a multi-unit polychord of mixed chordal construction.

Ex. 7-41

The polychordal combination of the triad with other chordal formations creates an additional and useful polychordal category. When combining chords by fourths with triads, place the triads below for linear freedom whether the fourths are perfect,

Ex. 7-42

or augmented.

Ex. 7-43

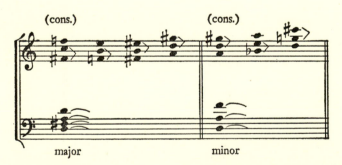

Triads are placed above for less resonant but useful subtle chords of a darker texture.

Ex. 7-44

Other polychordal combinations are possible.

Ex. 7-45

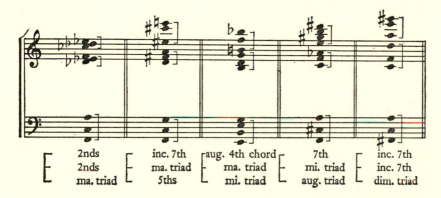

Source Material

Polychords, three or more units:

Arthur Honegger, Cris du Monde (red.), p. 9 (Senart)
Charles Ives, Piano Sonata No. 2, p. 26 (Arrow)
Olivier Messiaen, Visions de l'Amen, for two pianos, p. 2 (Durand)
Darius Milhaud, Cinq Symphonies (petit orchestre), p. 52 (Universal)
Humphrey Searle, Symphony No. 2, p. 38 (Schott)

Polychords, mixed units:

Béla Bartók, Sonata No. 2 for Violin and Piano, p. 29 (Universal)
Alban Berg, Wozzeck (red.), p. 71 (Universal)
Aaron Copland, Piano Fantasy, pp. 5–6 (Boosey)
Paul Hindemith, Piano Sonata No. 2, p. 12 (Schott)
Jacques Ibert, Divertissement, p. 52 (Durand)
Leon Kirchner, Duo for Violin and Piano, p. 9 (Mercury)
Marcel Mihalovici, Sinfonia Partita (strings), p. 62 (Heugel)
Darius Milhaud, Les Choëphores (red.), p. 41 (Heugel)
Arnold Schoenberg, De Profundis, p. 23 (Leeds)
Igor Stravinsky, Symphony in Three Movements, p. 11 (Associated)
Ernst Toch, The Princess and the Pea (red.), p. 26 (Schott)

Applications

1. Harmonize the following two-part passage in six-part polychords for the piano.

Ex. 7-46

2. Harmonize the following first-trumpet melody in six-part brass harmony (three trumpets and three trombones). Use a predominantly polychordal texture with occasional unison relief.

Ex. 7-47

3. Harmonize the following bass line for string sextet (two violins, two violas, and two cellos).

Ex. 7-48

4. Extend the polychordal passage for piano:

Ex. 7-49

5. Extend the woodwind passage featuring polychordal ornamentation.

Ex. 7-50

6. Extend the passage of broken polychords (three units) for piano.

Ex. 7-51

7. Continue the polychordal orchestral tutti.

Ex. 7-52

8. Additional lines for polychordal harmonization in any medium.

Ex. 7-53

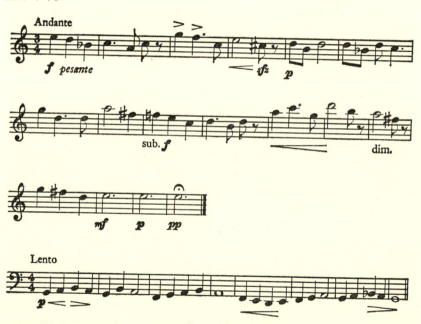

CHAPTER
EIGHT | # Compound and Mirror Harmony

COMPOUND CONSTRUCTION

MANY CHORDS are constructed by superimposing intervals of the third, of the fourth, or of the second. Another type of chord is made by superimposing combinations of miscellaneous intervals. This simultaneous combination of mixed intervals, not arranged in polychordal units, is a compound chord. Compound harmony does not include the chords of miscellaneous intervals formed by inverting tertian, quartal, or secundal structures, because these chords retain their inherent root feeling. When many intervals are combined into a compound structure a resounding body of tones results that is particularly effective in the orchestra, band, and piano, four hands.

Any combination of varied intervals is possible in a compound chord and the larger heterogeneous selections are often effective through sheer energy and tonal intensity:

Ex. 8-1

Intervals may be arranged in any combination of tensions. They may be distributed so as to produce any desired shape and assembled to create various consonant or dissonant areas. The combination of consonant or dissonant intervals may create a consonant or dissonant bottom, middle, or top portion of the chord.

Ex. 8-2

Some compound chords are characterized by an inner graphic plan rather than an arrangement of interval tensions. The important aspect of a chord of this kind is the logic of its inner construction rather than the motivating force of intervallic tension. Some such chords contain all twelve chromatic tones and eleven symmetrically invertible intervals.

Ex. 8-3

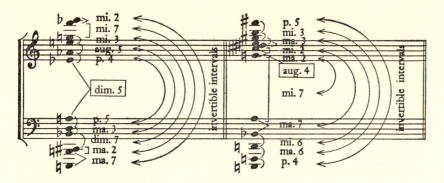

Other chords of this kind are arranged in alternately odd- or even-numbered intervals counted in semitones.

Ex. 8-4

Many other graphic interval arrangements are possible. Some chords are fashioned in the image of the overtone series. A pyramidal type of compound chord is composed of a series of intervals diminishing from the bottom upward.

Ex. 8-5

This pyramidal type may contain all twelve intervals but not necessarily twelve different notes.

Ex. 8-6

The polyinterval texture of compound chords enables harmonic areas of the chord to shift easily in any direction. Compound harmony progresses well when the chordal materials function under a definite scheme of intervallic tension. For example, passages may emphasize soft consonant and mild dissonant intervals at the top of the chord and open consonant and sharp dissonant intervals at the bottom.

Ex. 8-7

Passages may emphasize upper sharp dissonances and lower open consonances. If the upper tone of a sharp dissonant interval is placed high in the chord and anchored a fifth or tenth below, tension and brilliance are added.

Ex. 8-8

Smaller compound chords of five or six discreetly placed tones have an elastic quality because of the fluidity of the smaller number of varied intervals.

Ex. 8-9

Occasionally it will be difficult to decide whether certain chords are compound or added-note chords. A satisfactory analysis can be made only by examining the context of the harmony. If the chord in question shows strong tendencies to progress in a tonal sphere, it is an added-note chord containing notes that modify the basic structure of tonal functional powers; otherwise the chord is compound.

Compound chords do not readily subordinate themselves to the tonal regulation of root movement or key. Compound chords have little or no root significance and are usually handled simply as masses of sound. There is no likely scale to dominate the harmony and few harmonic values that result from relationships within a tonality. Any compound structure may be established as a central chord by the relative tension set up by surrounding chords, and may serve as the harmonic center to which adjacent chords gravitate.

Harmonic motion is created by the fluctuating density contained within the highest and lowest voices and by the shifting degrees of intervallic tension. The changing speeds with which the density and consonant-dissonant factors move create a harmonic rhythm in which compound chords may progress.

Compound chords are often large and complex and when used in succession are effective as declamations, arrival points, and opening and closing statements. They form naturally percussive chords when the smaller intervals are low in the structure.

Ex. 8-10

The inflexibility of large formations often limits their harmonic activity to percussive accentuations, sustained backgrounds, and cadences. When these chords are used for percussive accentuation two textural levels of different kinds may be created. The harmony containing the percussive chords is compound and the other may be tertian, quartal, or secundal.

Ex. 8-11

Compound chords may move as a background texture with no harmonic hold on a voice or voices in a solo foreground.

Ex. 8-12

In cadential treatment the compound chord of arrival is usually preceded by a structure of greater chordal density. The chords that lead to the final chords of the cadence are not necessarily compound.

Ex. 8-13

Because of the complexity of intervallic make-up in compound harmony each chordal member must be manipulated precisely. The slightest miscalculation can upset the intended balance. When care is given aurally to interval and medium color, a homogeneous and intelligible sonority may evolve.

One of the most frequently used compound chords is the three-note chord by fourths with the addition of a third (discussed in Chapter 4). Harmonically, this chord is flexible and colorful and functions well in tertian or quartal context.

A special category of compound chords stems from the triad with added seconds placed in the bass. When formations from this hybrid category (added-note chord and polychord) are written in open position a unique type of fused, compound harmony is produced. It is possible to fuse two triads so that a single chord of mixed intervals results. This species of compound harmony has a distinct polychordal flavor. Chords are formed by fusing two different kinds of triads so that two of the six notes are duplications, leaving a four-note formation. The duplicated notes are in the middle voices and are common to both triads. The chord is labeled from the bottom triad upwards.

Ex. 8-14

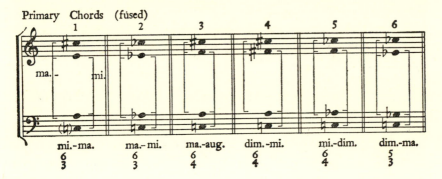

Primary Chords (fused)

There are only six compound chords of this variety; other fused combinations of triads form seventh or triadic harmony. These six fused chords are completely interchangeable and are free to move to and from each other in any order. They are, in effect, the six primary chords of this category. Their secondary chords are not compound and include those seventh, ninth, and eleventh chords in root position or inversion that contain a sharp dissonant interval which serves as a blending agent. These formations are numerous.

Ex. 8-15

Secondary Chords

Fused harmony flows freely in four parts.

Ex. 8-16

cadence   cadence
to secondary   to primary

Source Material

Compound harmony:

Easley Blackwood, Symphony No. 1, p. 48 (Elkan-Vogel)
Pierre Boulez, Piano Sonata No. 2, p. 3 (Heugel)
Benjamin Britten, The Turn of the Screw (red.), pp. 174, 181 (Boosey)
Elliott Carter, String Quartet No. 1, p. 29 (Associated)
Charles Ives, Piano Sonata No. 2, p. 42 (Arrow)
Arnold Schoenberg, Klavierstück Op. 33a, p. 2 (Universal)
William Schuman, Symphony No. 6, pp. 1, 49 (G. Schirmer)
Nikos Skalkottas, Little Suite for Strings, p. 10 (Kalmus)
Karlheinz Stockhausen, Kontra-Punkte, p. 39 (Universal)
Igor Stravinsky, Le Sacre du Printemps, p. 83 (Kalmus)
Edgard Varèse, Octandre, p. 11 (Ricordi)
Anton Webern, Kantate Op. 29, p. 1 (Universal)

MIRROR WRITING

Any chord (tertian, quartal, secundal, polychordal, or compound) may be mirrored by adding below the original formation strictly inverted intervals in symmetrical reflection. One half of a mirror chord is an exact and simultaneous inversion of the other half. Mirror harmony has a textural complexion unlike any other chordal formation because reflective inversion opposes the natural

acoustical properties of sound, in that the overtones that form the
character of a single tone are naturally generated from the bottom,
not from the middle, as in a mirror. The spurious undertone series,
an intervallic reflection of the overtone series, is the only instance
of a mirror as a natural musical phenomenon and is theoretical
rather than aural.

Ex. 8-17

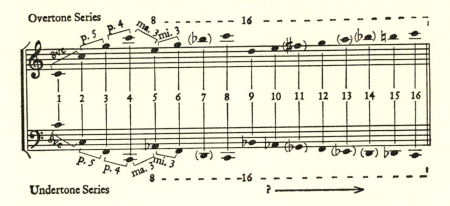

In mirror harmony, fundamental chords by thirds, fourths, and
seconds generate larger formations of the same category. Mirroring
inverted chords produces polychords, and mirroring polychords
and compound chords produces more complex versions of the
same kind of structure.

Ex. 8-18

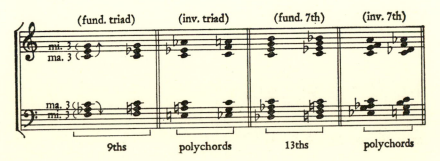

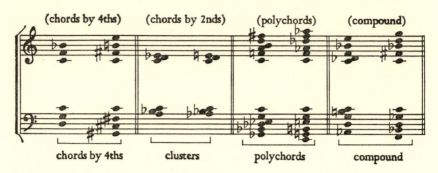

Four possible types of mirror chord writing are: a stationary building tone used to generate reflection (*a*); a moving building tone generating reflection (*b*); the building tones themselves becoming reflective by moving in contrary motion (*c*); building tones used freely (*d*).

Ex. 8-19

Any mirror chord may be doubly mirrored. These complex
structures are used primarily with large unmirrored compound
chords. Enharmonic changes are made when spelling becomes unwieldy.

Ex. 8-20

Even though the members of mirror chords are built from a
tone or tones located in the center of the chord the building tone
never functions aurally as a root. It is the entire chordal bulk that
emerges as a chord in its own right. Mirror chords usually assume
the character of the bottom chord.

Some scales are naturally reflective in that two separate scales
move identically, interval for interval, when placed in contrary
motion. The entire diatonic scale system is symmetrically invertible. The mirrored diatonic scales appear in a reversed order of
color gradation. The dorian in mirrored version produces the
same scale.

Ex. 8-21

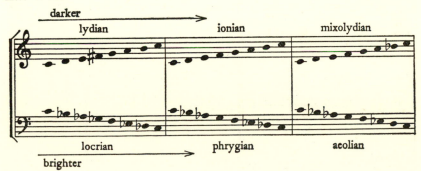

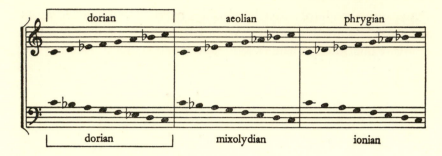

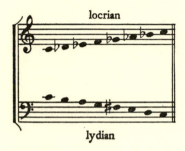

Any scale may be reflected. The following illustrates synthetic scale mirroring.

Ex. 8-22

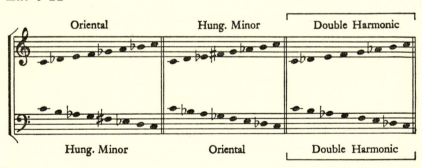

Some synthetic scales, such as the Double Harmonic, are inversely identical.

Reflective scales imply mirror harmony.

Ex. 8-23

Reflective scales whose tonics are located at different pitch levels also produce mirror chords. The flavor of each chord of reflective harmony becomes more pronounced as the space between the building tones widens.

Ex. 8-24

When strict mirror writing is desired, ornamental tones are kept in reflective relationship:

Ex. 8-25

Greater freedom in harmony can be obtained through only partial reflection, the outer voices mirrored while the inner voices move freely.

Ex. 8-26

Mirror writing may stem from thematic sources; an initial melody can be constructed so that part of the melody is the inversion of another part. Subsequent simultaneous use of the original melody and its inversion breeds mirrored vertical structures generated by the thematic elements of the work.

Ex. 8-27

Reflective keyboard writing produces unique mirror harmony that equalizes the movement of the hands and creates simultaneous and uniform keyboard technique. When musically appropriate, reflective keyboard passages supply a fresh sound. The mirror or reflective pivotal points of the keyboard are D and G♯. Corresponding notes in the keyboard mirror are these:

D D♯ E F F♯ G G♯ A A♯ B C C♯ (D)
D C♯ C B A♯ A G♯ G F♯ F E D♯ (D)

Simultaneous inversion beginning at any one of the twelve pivotal points produces strict mirroring regardless of what type of harmony is used; the fingering in both hands will, without exception, be identical:

Ex. 8-28

Source Material

Mirror writing:

Béla Bartók, Concerto for Orchestra, p. 1 (Boosey)
Karl-Birger Blomdahl, Chamber Concerto (red.), p. 17 (Schott)
Aaron Copland, Vitebsk (violin, cello, and piano), p. 2 (Cos Cob)
Luigi Dallapiccola, Quaderno Musicale di Annalibera (piano), p. 9 (Zerboni)
Karl Amadeus Hartmann, Concerto for Piano, Winds, and Percussion, pp. 32–33 (Schott)
Darius Milhaud, Les Choëphores (red.), pp. 10, 76 (Heugel)
Vincent Persichetti, Sixth Piano Sonata, p. 18 (Elkan-Vogel)
George Rochberg, Duo Concertante for Violin and Cello, p. 13 (Presser)
Gerald Strang, Mirrorrorrim (New Music)
Alexandre Tansman, Petite Suite, p. 7 (Demets)
Antonio Veretti, Piano Sonatina, p. 19 (Ricordi)

Applications

1. Write a section of a two-piano piece including the following compound chords in any order and in any transposition.

Ex. 8-29

2. Write an orchestral passage containing a sequence having for its harmonic background a progression of heterogeneous compound chords.

3. Write a passage for winds that includes several pyramidal chords.

4. Write a turbulent passage of tertian harmony for a chamber group in which large compound chords are used for percussive accentuation.

5. Write a compound chordal section for oboe, clarinet, horn, and bassoon in which fused chords are employed.

6. Write music for two clarinets with simultaneous mirroring.

7. Move a chamber group through several mirror chords where the reflective harmony is generated by the same tone and by different tones.

8. Write an opening section of a two-part piece for the piano employing two symmetrically invertible scales. The mirror writing should be kept strict throughout.

9. Illustrate reflective keyboard writing in a short allegro section for piano.

| Harmonic Direction

PROGRESSION

WHEN A SUCCESSION of chords establishes a definite direction it
has formal function and is considered a progression. The goal of a
progression may be reached or abandoned, a tonality fixed or for-
saken.

Whether a succession of chords is established by root movement,
contrapuntal lines, or beds of sound, the composer is able to guide
his harmony in any direction. In root progression, inverted or
otherwise, there are two directional factors: action of the root
and location of the bass. The root, not necessarily in the bass, may
fall as the sounding bass rises, or rise as the sounding bass falls,
or the factors may agree in direction.

Ex. 9-1

Melodic and harmonic lines of tension may be placed in variable relationships with the root movement.

Ex. 9-2

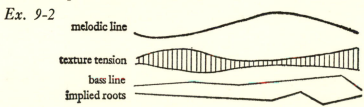

Although register placement of the entire tonal mass does affect the direction of sound,

Ex. 9-3

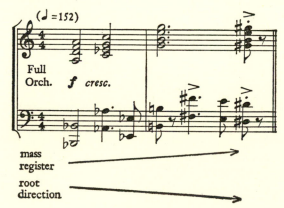

harmony with a strong downward pull can resist a register climb.

Ex. 9-4

Progressions based upon the interval of the perfect fifth between roots have strength; those based upon the third, softness; upon the second, blandness; and upon the tritone, ambiguity (notice that these intervals together subsume all twelve tones).

Ex. 9-5

The root direction of I-V, I-III, and I-II is up, regardless of the inversion or placement of voices. The root direction of I-IV, I-VI, and I-VII is down. The uninvertible tritone is indefinite as to direction.

In tonal music of the twentieth century, the root distance between important chords of a phrase or cadence is usually determined by the cycle upon which the music is constructed. Music in a cyclical fifth relationship is governed by a series of perfect fifths which may encompass the twelve different tones (*a*). In a third relationship the chromatic compass is created by alternating major and minor thirds (*b*). In cyclical second relationship a series of major and minor seconds is used to encircle the twelve tones (*c*).

Ex. 9-6

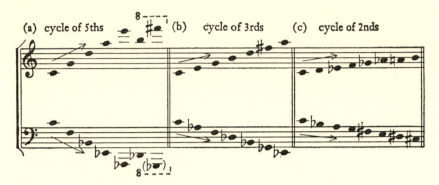

Harmonic writing, then, may be based upon the fifth, third, or second relationship of chords (simple or complex), upon the tension created by moving from one kind of relationship to another, or simply upon the horizontal movement of voices.

Chordal relationships may be established within or without a prevailing scale formation and a tension created by moving from one to another. Chordal movement in which the intervals between the roots are chromatically free is not governed by a scale but by horizontal movement of the voices.

Harmonic movement may be created by generous chromaticism in all the voices and the emphasis placed upon a total melodic motion obliterating intervallic construction of chords. In augmented triads, diminished seventh chords, chords by perfect fourths or major seconds, roots are indefinite and vanish quickly. These versatile chords link one kind of texture to another while acting as binding chords in a synthesis of harmonic contexts.

A melodic line, whether an inner or outer voice, often acts as a directional guide for harmonic progression. When a complex melody is the motivating force, the success of motivic development depends upon the ability of the ear to retain melodic elements. Predominant intervals and durations must be aurally retainable, and those elements that have special significance for the formal plan should be made melodic and harmonic characteristics. Melodies imply tonal inflection, harmonic punctuation, and rhythmic movement, and any one of these elements may be featured. The composer is constantly aware of culminating points, general design, articulation, phrasing, dynamics, the rhythmic meaning of each note, predominant interval textures, and characteristics of the medium.

Other factors must be considered in creating harmonic progression: the textural influence of intervals characteristic of specific types of harmony, the effect of frequently occurring melodic motifs upon harmonic phrase shapes, the behavior of the tritone in both horizontal and vertical situations, the placement of chords in a presiding or vanishing tonal center, and the recovery of harmonic equilibrium after swift changes of compositional devices.

A vital thematic passage should be tested on various tonal levels for brilliance. Transposition sheds varying lights upon thematic material; the slightest shift in register can change the meaning of a musical idea.

When writing music without a given line, attention should be focused upon the outer voices. If undecided about upper voice motion, work a few notes ahead in the bass, and vice versa. If parts begin moving too fast, slow down most of the parts with longer notes and move the remaining part or parts by employing a fragment of the theme.

The following examples illustrate special kinds of chordal movement. A succession consisting of an interchange of two or three chords may be used for "atmospheric" passages where neither definite tonality nor forward harmonic motion is desired,

Ex. 9-7

or for music with folk roots.

Ex. 9-8

Any chord can return to the chord that immediately precedes it (*a*); and succeeding chords may return to an original formation (*b*).

Ex. 9-9

An entire passage of chords may be stated backwards until the original chord reappears. Retrogressive progressions bring new meaning to the original harmonic statement.

Ex. 9-10

Unexpected chords at resolution points add freshness to harmonic flow:

Ex. 9-11

Harmonic elision brings about new relationships. Chordal relationships new to the piece may appear by omitting a chord that is expected because of previously established passages or strong sequential or traditional successions.

Ex. 9-12

If a passage is thematically significant and is easily retained aurally, chords may be omitted or shuffled in a dismembered progression.

Ex. 9-13

CHORD CONNECTION

Two inseparable factors are involved with harmonic progression: what chord follows what chord, and how they are connected. When melodies sound together chords are formed, and when chords follow each other melodic motion is involved. Music can be primarily harmonic, melodic, or rhythmic, but there is seldom pure harmony or counterpoint for they are deeply involved with each other. Separate chord tones of any progression have melodic tendencies; even the most isolated chord is full of melodic potential.

Outer voices govern harmonic direction and inner voices secure the relationship of the chords. For unruffled harmonic motion inner voices are moved as little as possible and common tones are held. Parallel intervals lessen the individuality of the voices and contrary and oblique motion give the voices independence. The inherent urge of independent voices to maintain identifiable lines can be strong enough to overpower harmonic impulse.

Smooth progressions are but one facet of the craft. There is a danger of their becoming overly smooth and much ingenuity is required to keep them fresh. Leaping voices, straying dissonances, escaping common tones, modulatory twists, and chromatic daring are all part of harmonic technique.

The following devices help give harmonic writing this freshness. Inverting or transposing the interval containing common tones expands the register range:

Ex. 9-14

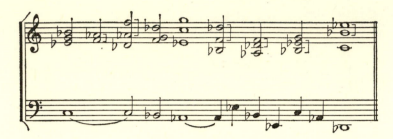

Moving a voice to a note higher than the one just left by the voice above, or to a note lower than the note just left by the voice below, gives a passage a harmonic lift or drop.

Ex. 9-15

A voice may be animated by deflecting its melodic line, one or more of the melody notes being shifted up or down an octave.

Ex. 9-16

The register of an entire harmonic mass may be shifted suddenly to another octave.

Ex. 9-17

The range suppleness of instruments may contribute to linear flexibility.

Ex. 9-18

Melodic rises and dips may be reinforced by successive octaves, fifths, and parallel harmony.

Ex. 9-19

Hidden fifths and octaves give coupled two-part harmony textural strength, and thirdless harmony a freedom of movement.

Ex. 9-20

The number of voices in successive chords may be increased or decreased for variety in density.

Ex. 9-21

A climactic harmonic point may be left vacant by rests.

Ex. 9-22

Voices may take turns sounding the tune. When voices share a melody in this way thematic implications are felt in the harmony.

Ex. 9-23

Each voice may move chromatically to daringly complex chords because when all voices move by half step any combination of dissonances may have meaning and direction. The voices containing the sharpest dissonant interval should be well separated:

Ex. 9-24

DISSONANCE

Any combination of simultaneously sounding tones is relatively consonant if there is a more dissonant combination in the surrounding area. An abundance of dissonance can result in the feeling of a consonant texture because the harmonic tension often relaxes in chords of the same values. The juxtaposition of chords of different values creates strong harmonic tension. A chord is dissonant only in relation to an over-all harmonic scheme and at times the "consonant" chord is the restless one. Because of melodic pull and chordal relationships the "consonant" chord at (*a*) has a strong urge to move while the "dissonant" chord at (*b*) remains unflustered.

Ex. 9-25

Increasing and decreasing consonance or dissonance contributes to the shape of phrases, secures cadential progressions, and articulates sectional writing. Some are inherently more dissonant than others. But from the esthetic point of view the composer's ear determines interval consonance or dissonance. Dissonance exists only where there is a norm of consonance implied or stated. A ninth chord may be relatively dissonant and restless because of the less dissonant seventh and triadic material surrounding it, but the same ninth might be perfectly secured in consonance in a context of ninths, elevenths, and polychords.

Consonant-dissonant relationship may be reversed by starting and ending with a dissonant chord as the norm; consonance may then resolve to dissonance. Extremely dissonant chords are kept in check by sequential patterns, overbearing melodic lines, and characteristic melodic intervals. A dissonant chord might represent a tonality and generate ideas that suggest the form and content of a large work.

A dissonant chord has special uses outside a dissonant context. It sometimes ends a phrase when used to begin the next phrase (transposed or not),

Ex. 9-26

or is repeated so dynamically and intensely that the need for resolution is eradicated.

In harmonic progression, each note makes its position in the chord felt as well as its position in its own melodic line. This linear force generates the harmony, contrapuntal motion, and formal design. Dissonant melodic and chordal clashes occur with less aural concern in harmony stemming from horizontal thinking—in multi-voice counterpoint (counterchords), in ornamental chords, and in reflection of some of the voices.

Dissonant harmonic combinations often produce a diatonic melody.

Ex. 9-27

This melodic writing must not be confused with artificial combinations of diatonic melody and dissonant harmony.

When a chord is dissonant by context it is usually resolved by the movement of the voices containing the most dissonant tones. For smoothness of progression the dissonant tone resolves to the nearest note of the prevailing scale scheme.

Ex. 9-28

The dissonant tone can resist its natural tendency to move to the nearest note by following a scalewise motion in the opposite direction. If the adjacent scale tones are the same distance from the dissonant tone, movement in either direction is natural. For passive non-commitment it remains stationary, or leaps an octave at the chord change.

Ex. 9-29

A dissonant tone may evaporate by skipping to another member of the same chord or may freeze in parallel harmony and not resolve until the end of the passage. The dissonant tone may skip freely with melodic purpose in high-tension mixed chordal formations or when strong melodic motifs overshadow the power of the dissonant tone to resolve. The momentum of sequential design moves dissonant tones without resolution. For a sudden tension lift, the dissonant tone may resolve in another voice.

Ex. 9-30

The quality of the dissonant tone can be softened by coupling it with consonant intervals, but doubling of the dissonant tone raises the harmonic tension. Such doubling in a simple chord enables that chord to function easily with complex formations.

Ex. 9-31

To soften doubled dissonant tones, the voices involving the dissonance move in contrary motion, or one of the doubled tones may move before the other resolves.

The spacing concern in three- and four-part harmony is often one of securing maximum sound, but in harmony of more than four parts, doubling and spacing considerations are directed to securing variety of texture. Various colors and weights are obtainable through omission and doubling of both dissonant and consonant chord members. The density and concentration of tonal sound varies under different dramatic conditions. In an orchestral arrival of dissonant material upon a consonant climax, extensive doubling of all members of the consonant chord may be necessary to avoid loss of sound.

PARALLEL HARMONY

When all voices in a succession of chords move in the same direction, parallel harmony occurs. Parallel harmony is found in eighteenth-century six-three successions and in nineteenth-century diminished seventh chord successions. The term includes both strict parallel motion in which all the chords are identical in construction, and similar motion in which the chords change as the voices move freely but in the same direction. The direction and intervallic transpositions may vary and be either real or tonal.

Ex. 9-32

Real parallel harmony (exact transposition) has a tendency to sever connections with any one key and may be used as a means of entering and leaving atonality. This kind of harmony functions freely in modulatory transitions and in thematic statements where tonality is meant to be obscure. Tonal parallel harmony (intervallic changes determined by the scale in force) tends to preserve a modality.

Parallel harmony (or chordal melody) is an expanded textural equivalent of a melodic line; its direction is governed primarily by melodic considerations and its intervallic construction by the kind of texture demanded by the dramatic form. In parallel harmony, fourths and fifths are as liquid as thirds and sixths, and intervals of the second and seventh find horizontal freedom.

Momentary parallel harmony is effective when used to accentuate a rise or fall in a melodic line or to slip into a fresh key area. But extended similar motion tires quickly even though complex chords are employed. Ways to develop the generating force of parallel harmony have become part of the composer's craft. Before parallel harmony becomes monotonous one of the following devices may be employed for a renewal of harmonic freshness and flow: contrary motion in one voice against the current parallel succession (*a*); tonal parallel motion converted to real (*b*);

Ex. 9-33

motion of the voices changed to similar motion (*a*); the roots of parallel chords moved in the direction opposite to the moving mass (*b*);

Ex. 9-34

the direction and register changed (*a*); notes dropped while the parallel harmony is continued (*b*);

Ex. 9-35

attention diverted by ornamentation and imitation (*a*); the octave changed in one voice (*b*);

Ex. 9-36

the instrumentation changed (*a*); different instruments used on different notes (*b*);

Ex. 9-37

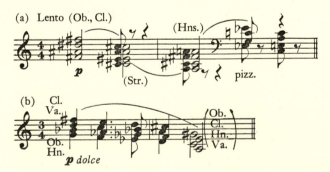

all notes raised or dropped successively until the chord is duplicated at some other step.

Ex. 9-38

Str. *p a bene placido*

Parallel harmony may be relieved by inserting fragments of non-
parallel harmony, or by using two sets of parallel chords in
contrary motion—the result may or may not be reflective.

The chordal formation that dominates a succession of parallel
chords may be broken melodically and a new set of parallel chords
placed under the melodic notes of the broken chord, resulting in
oblique harmony.

Ex. 9-39

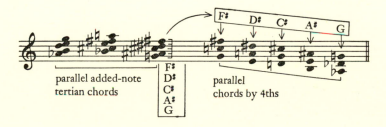

parallel added-note
tertian chords

parallel
chords by 4ths

SUCCESSIVE PERFECT FIFTHS

Unless used imaginatively, successive perfect fifths become
tiresome; the intervallic uniformity of any combination of notes
moving in parallel motion challenges a composer's inventiveness
and facility. Fifths are emotionally immense, vague, and distant,
or bare and dominating—they form an important harmonic in-

gredient in contemporary composition. They are found in two-part writing, prying loose oblique motion;

Ex. 9-40

in coupled two-part writing;

Ex. 9-41

in parallel harmony;

Ex. 9-42

at the end of one sequential pattern and the beginning of the next;

Ex. 9-43

and at phrase joints.

Ex. 9-44

Although perfect fifths make independence of parts difficult to achieve, their function in the vast tonal reserve is an important one. As part of a moving chordal body of sound they can be used without dominating the general texture. The following devices help push perfect fifths to the background. Conjunct fifths may be placed in the lower voices while other parts employ contrary or oblique motion.

Ex. 9-45

Fifths in the upper parts become prominent but attention may be diverted by using rhythmically agile accompanying parts.

Ex. 9-46

Chromatic fifths may be used more freely if at least one voice moves contrary to the fifths (*a*). Some monotony can be avoided by inserting other intervals between some of the fifths (*b*).

Ex. 9-47

Contrary outer parts may be used with fifths in the inner parts (*a*). Fifths in the upper parts are softened by placing the third of the fifth in a lower voice (*b*).

Ex. 9-48

Skipping fifths are subdued when they leap to members of the same chord (*a*). Florid inner voices help divert the attention from fifths in the outer parts (*b*).

Ex. 9-49

CADENTIAL DEVICES

A cadence is an organization of melody and harmony in time, having a connotation of rest. The cadence is created harmonically through a pattern of chords, and melodically through the direction of each voice. Both are positive forces only when verified rhythmically. Cadential breathing places may occur at ends of phrases and sections and finally at the end of the piece. Under certain formal conditions, however, the final cadence may find that a prominent subject in a different key has made a bid for a new tonality, causing a cadence of two or more simultaneous keys.

Regardless of the complexity or inversions of the cadential chords, the two final roots will set the quality of the cadential feeling. The first chord in a two-chord cadence progresses "perfectly" to a tonic whose root lies the interval of the existing cyclical relationship below its own.

Ex. 9-50

The plagal equivalents are these:

Ex. 9-51

Any cadence will acquire a passive quality if a dissonant tone remains stationary.

Ex. 9-52

Tension and relaxation of consonance and dissonance help mold cadential shapes. However, a succession of chords can produce positive cadential finality only when the underlying rhythm confirms them. The rhythmic placement of the final chord affects the strength of the cadence; when the last chord falls on a weak beat, repeated notes, ties, or melodic ornamentation are used to regain balance.

Ex. 9-53

In chromatic cadences, common tones are avoided in order to strengthen the final tonic footing.

Ex. 9-54

The purpose of temporary cadences is to rest briefly on a harmonic slant, thereby creating a need for harmonic, rhythmic, and melodic continuance. Deceptive cadences are usually of this type and imply motion from one chord to another whose root relation to the first forms an interval not characteristic of the prevailing chordal cycle. In fifth relationship, the chord of weaker impulse moves to a chord whose root lies a second above its own root (*a*). In third relationship, root movement is up five (*b*). In second relationship, root movement is up three (*c*).

Ex. 9-55

Deceptive cadential progressions are also obtained through movement to a chord outside the established modal or key realm, or by chromatic root movement. Other cadences are created by the obliteration of all voices but one, or obliteration of all voices save a percussion note of indefinite pitch.

When the final tonic establishes a positive tonality, notes may be added freely, and if undertones are added, the tonic meaning is not disturbed. The final chord may be identical with the opening chord regardless of tonal relationships.

Cadences may include any type of harmony: tertian, quartal, added-note, secundal, polychordal, compound, mirror, pandiatonic (Chapter 10), or twelve-note.

Ex. 9-56

Source Material

Harmony with characteristic doubling, spacing, or omission:

Aaron Copland, Piano Sonata, pp. 5, 29 (Boosey)
Darius Milhaud, Protée (red.), p. 86 (Durand)
Luigi Nono, Incontri for 24 Instruments, p. 14 (Scherchen)
Igor Stravinsky, Mass, p. 13 (Boosey)
Anton Webern, Kantate Op. 31, p. 3 (Universal)

Retrogressive writing:

Béla Bartók, Music for String Instruments, Percussion, and Celesta, p. 14
    (Boosey)
Alban Berg, Lyric Suite, pp. 39–45 (Universal)
Luigi Dallapiccola, Quaderno Musicale di Annalibera (piano), p. 11
    (Zerboni)
Paul Hindemith, Ludus Tonalis, pp. 13–14, 57–60 (Associated)
Olivier Messiaen, Sept Pièces pour Orgue, pp. 3–4 (Leduc)
Darius Milhaud, The Household Muse, p. 14 (Elkan-Vogel)
Anton Webern, Variationen Op. 27, p. 3 (Universal)

Real parallel harmony:

Niels Viggo Bentzon, String Quartet No. 3, p. 11 (Hansen)
Alban Berg, Wozzeck (red.), p. 219–221 (Universal)
George Gershwin, An American in Paris, p. 48 (Harms)
Karl Amadeus Hartmann, Konzert für Bratsche mit Klavier, p. 3 (Schott)
André Jolivet, Piano Concerto (red.), p. 42 (Heugel)
Roger Sessions, Symphony No. 2, p. 99 (G. Schirmer)
Ralph Vaughan Williams, Pastoral Symphony, p. 49 (Boosey)

Tonal parallel harmony:

Elliott Carter, Variations for Orchestra, p. 52 (Associated)
Goffredo Petrassi, Toccata for Piano, p. 5 (Ricordi)
Francis Poulenc, Les Soirées de Nazelles (piano), p. 19 (Durand)
Igor Stravinsky, Le Sacre du Printemps, p. 39 (Kalmus)
Virgil Thomson, Four Saints in Three Acts (red.), p. 139 (Arrow)

Altered parallel writing:

Béla Bartók, Piano Concerto No. 2 (red.), p. 38 (Boosey)
Alban Berg, Lyric Suite, pp. 12, 25 (Universal)
John Alden Carpenter, Skyscrapers (red.), p. 39 (G. Schirmer)
Frederick Delius, Requiem (red.), p. 54 (Universal)
Roy Harris, Symphony No. 7, p. 89 (Associated)
Maurice Ravel, L'Heure Espagnole (red.), p. 113 (Durand)
Henri Sauguet, Concerto d'Orphée (red.), p. 38 (Heugel)
Igor Stravinsky, Perséphone (red.), p. 29 (Russe)
Hugo Weisgall, The Tenor (red.), p. 145 (Merion)

Passages of bare fifths:

Georges Auric, Les Facheux (red.), p. 14 (Lerolle)
Aaron Copland, Billy the Kid (ballet suite), p. 1 (Boosey)
Manuel de Falla, Nuits dans les Jardins d'Espagne (red.), p. 17 (Eschig)
Roy Harris, Symphony No. 3, p. 1 (G. Schirmer)
Gian Carlo Menotti, The Unicorn, the Gorgon and the Manticore (red.),
    p. 44 (Ricordi)
William Schuman, Symphony No. 3, p. 70 (G. Schirmer)

Harmony containing perfect fifths:

Alberto Ginastera, Piano Sonata, p. 7 (Barry)
Roy Harris, Piano Quintet, pp. 8–9 (G. Schirmer)
Bernhard Heiden, Sonata for Horn and Piano, p. 14 (Associated)
Paul Hindemith, Ludus Tonalis, p. 15 (Schott)
Charles Ives, Piano Sonata No. 1, p. 21 (Peer)
Dane Rudhyar, Three Paeans for Piano, p. 6 (New Music)
William Schuman, Credendum, p. 12 (Presser)
Roger Sessions, Piano Sonata No. 2, p. 8 (Marks)
Halsey Stevens, Quintet for Flute, Violin, Viola, Cello and Piano, p. 1
    (G. Schirmer for S.P.A.M.)
Igor Stravinsky, Les Noces, p. 36 (Chester)
Stefan Wolpe, Passacaglia for Piano, p. 8 (New Music)

Characteristic cadences:

Pierre Boulez, Piano Sonata No. 2, p. 15 (Heugel)
Carlos Chávez, Sinfonia India, p. 82 (G. Schirmer)
Aaron Copland, Music for the Theatre, p. 67 (Boosey)

Andrew Imbrie, Piano Sonata, p. 9 (Valley)
Bruno Maderna, Serenata No. 2 (for 11 instruments), p. 54 (Zerboni)
Francis Poulenc, Mass in G major, p. 24 (Rouart-Lerolle)
Arnold Schoenberg, Erwartung (red.), p. 47 (Universal)
Gunther Schuller, Contours (small orchestra), p. 99 (Schott)
Camillo Togni, Fantasia Concertante (flute and strings), p. 38 (Zerboni)
Ilhan Usmanbas, String Quartet, p. 31 (Boosey)
Roman Vlad, Sonatina for Flute and Piano, p. 18 (Zerboni)
Ben Weber, Serenade for Strings, p. 24 (Boosey)

Applications

1. Write a sustained passage for organ in which the melodic and harmonic lines of tension are in variable relationships with the root movement.

2. Write an arioso for viola and piano (or harpsichord) in which the entire circle of thirds is covered by transient keys.

3. Write a chromatic lamentation for strings where emphasis upon total melodic motion obliterates root feeling.

4. Shed varying lights upon thematic orchestral material by shifting the register several times.

5. Write an extended succession consisting of only three chords for four saxophones (AAT and Bar).

6. Write a woodwind chorale featuring retrogressive progressions.

7. Shuffle the chords of a passage so that pizzicato strings can project a dismembered progression.

8. Write a martial section for winds featuring leaping voices, straying dissonances, escaping common tones, modulatory twists, and chromatic daring.

9. Write an abundance of dissonance for the chamber orchestra so that a relatively consonant texture emerges.

10. Write an orchestral variation on a folk tune featuring various parallel harmony devices.

11. Place a great number of perfect fifths in the background of an agile dance for two pianos and brasses.

12. Write a guitar or harp piece with several tempo changes and different kinds of cadences.

| Timing and Dynamics

RHYTHM

THREE FORCES important to harmonic progression are the linear motion and outline of outer voices, the pull of harmonic or tonal centers and of the relationship of chords, and the time duration of stressed and unstressed chords. Coupled with these forces are graded tensions of texture and pitch and the rhythm created by phrasing, bowing, and tonguing indications.

Harmony is always felt in its relation to rhythmic structure, and not until chords evolve in a rhythmic form does harmony become wholly articulate. Harmonic rhythm is the underlying rhythm that plays a large part in controlling and stabilizing musical flow. If the harmonic changes are quick, there is an undercurrent of restlessness; if widely spaced, there is breadth. Various combinations of fluctuating melodic and harmonic rhythms give the composer a creative rhythmic potential.

Tempo can be a determining factor in harmonic rhythm. Quick tempo may cause chord changes to sound like ornamental chords. Simple chords moving at a high rate of speed may create relatively complex sounds (*a*). Harmonic rhythm does not move when chords are repeated (*b*).

Ex. 10-1

Meter is a measure of rhythm. It has no rhythm of its own; it only appears to have when rhythmic pulse coincides with the metric points. Strong and weak beats occur wherever the musical line places them, regardless of meter.

Ex. 10-2

Simple rhythms may be combined under one time signature.

Ex. 10-3

If patterns of shifted accents remain relatively consistent the asymmetrical divisions are often indicated by compound time signatures or dotted lines. These composite meters generate asymmetrical phrases.

Two patterns of varying note values coinciding at occasional points will flow without a feeling of chaos.

Ex. 10-4

Two or more rhythmic phrases of unequal length may each be repeated until the return of the original combination (polyrhythm).

Ex. 10-5

etc.

When the pulse is irregularly but consistently subdivided, different time signatures are used simultaneously (polymeter).

Ex. 10-6

Complete rhythmic independence of voices is obtained by using different time signatures with bar lines falling at different places.

Ex. 10-7

Change of meter is a common means of achieving rhythmic variety. The fluid bar line adjusts easily and accommodates fractional measures. Rhythmic freedom of the bar line may result from the demands of vocal texts (prose rhythm).

Musical stress is created by pitch, intensity, color, or duration; the more factors contributing to an accent the more complete the accent. Rhythmic pulse is most clearly defined when the related melodic, contrapuntal, and harmonic functions are emphasized. Although syncopation implies a dislocation of an established pulse, it does not necessarily oppose the meter. If the established pulse is not in accord with the meter the syncopated accents might parallel the meter.

Ex. 10-8

syncopation

Any part of a rhythmic figure may be lengthened by a note (*a*), a rest (*b*), or a dot (*c*). The rhythmic transformation produces ametrical patterns:

Ex. 10-9

The melodic and harmonic lines may be syncopated in opposing ways: the melodic line syncopated against harmonic pulse, harmonic rhythm syncopated against melodic pulse, or both harmonic and melodic pulse heard in comparison with a contrasting pulse of preceding measures. Changes of time signature may be made so that the syncopation falls after the bar line. Dissonant-chord syncopations urge the succeeding harmonic rhythm to move faster and consonant-chord syncopations tend to slow it down.

Rhythmic forces may sprout from the percussion line of instruments or vocal sounds of indeterminate pitches. The melodic and harmonic rhythms may coincide or oppose the percussion line in various ways. The following example illustrates melodic and percussive rhythm opposing the harmonic rhythm.

Ex. 10-10

When one or more voices of changing notes adhere to a single rhythmic pattern, isorhythm exists.

Ex. 10-11

Different voices may follow individual isorhythmic patterns.

Ex. 10-12

Isorhythmic patterns may vary in length. When the pattern is ᵻ long one, the device is often beyond immediate aural perception.

In isorhythm, the pitch levels are free and used with a repeated rhythmic pattern, but when the rhythm is free with a repeated melodic pattern, a device called isomelos exists:

Ex. 10-13

In a combination of isorhythm and isomelos, the melodic and rhythmic patterns may start together, but one of the patterns may begin the repetition before the other.

Ex. 10-14

Source Material

Irregular harmonic rhythm:

Milton Babbitt, Three Compositions for Piano, p. 6 (Bomart)
Benjamin Britten, Serenade for Tenor, Horn and Strings, p. 34 (Boosey)
Jean Françaix, Piano Concerto (red.), p. 25 (Schott)
Paul Hindemith, Sonata for Viola and Piano, p. 15 (Schott)
André Jolivet, String Quartet No. 1, p. 26 (Heugel)
Ernst Krenek, Piano Sonata No. 4, p. 21 (Bomart)
Quincy Porter, String Quartet No. 8, p. 21 (Valley)
Serge Prokofiev, Piano Sonata No. 6, p. 17 (Am-Rus)
Arnold Schoenberg, Das Buch der Hängenden Gärten, p. 10 (Universal)

Meter changes:

John Becker, String Quartet No. 2, p. 9 (New Music)
Boris Blacher, Divertimento, p. 3 (Associated)
Aaron Copland, Sextet for String Quartet, Clarinet and Piano, p. 5 (Boosey)
Roman Haubenstock-Ramati, Les Symphonies de Timbres, pp. 10–11 (Universal)
Paul Hindemith, Neues vom Tage (red.), p. 198 (Schott)
Peter Mennin, String Quartet No. 2, p. 24 (C. Fischer)
Silvestre Revueltas, Sensemaya, pp. 27–37 (G. Schirmer)
Roger Sessions, Symphony No. 1, p. 7 (Arrow)

Polyrhythms:

Samuel Barber, Vanessa (red.), p. 172 (G. Schirmer)
Aaron Copland, Symphony No. 1, p. 20 (Cos Cob)
Charles Ives, Symphony No. 3, pp. 26–27 (Arrow)
Arnold Schoenberg, String Trio Op. 45, p. 13 (Bomart)
Gunther Schuller, String Quartet No. 1, p. 27 (Universal)
Alexander Scriabine, Tenth Piano Sonata, p. 2 (Leeds)
Karlheinz Stockhausen, Nr. 5 Zeitmasse, p. 21 (Universal)

Poly-time-signatures:

Béla Bartók, String Quartet No. 3, pp. 9, 23 (Boosey)
Jack Beeson, Five Songs, p. 6 (Peer)
Elliott Carter, String Quartet No. 1, p. 5 (Associated)
Paul Hindemith, Symphonie Mathis der Maler, pp. 20–22 (Schott)
Maurice Ravel, Sonate pour Violon et Violoncelle, p. 5 (Durand)
Igor Stravinsky, Petrushka, p. 10 (Kalmus)

Passages featuring percussive sounds:

Carlos Chávez, Toccata for Percussion Instruments (Affiliated)
Karl Amadeus Hartmann, Symphony No. 6, p. 102 (Schott)
Paul Hindemith, Symphonic Metamorphosis, p. 36 (Associated)
Gustav Holst, The Planets, p. 1 (Boosey)
Lev Knipper, Symphony No. 4, p. 49 (Leeds)
Luigi Nono, Coro di Didone, pp. 17, 23 (Ars Viva)
Silvestre Revueltas, Sensemaya, p. 25 (G. Schirmer)
Gunther Schuller, Contours (small orchestra), p. 19 (Schott)
Edgard Varèse, Density 21.5 (New Music)

Isorhythm and isomelos:

Samuel Barber, Piano Sonata, p. 38 (G. Schirmer)
Benjamin Britten, Peter Grimes (red.), p. 172 (Boosey)
Aaron Copland, Piano Sonata, p. 14 (Boosey)
Arthur Honegger, Cris du Monde (red.), p. 23 (Senart)
Peter Mennin, Symphony No. 3, pp. 128–129 (Hargail)
Burrill Phillips, Sonata for Cello and Piano, p. 31 (Wash. Univ.)
Walter Piston, Symphony No. 4, pp. 99–100 (Associated)
Alan Rawsthorne, Quartet for Clarinet, Violin, Viola and Cello, p. 17 (Oxford)
George Rochberg, Sonata-Fantasia for Piano, p. 18 (Presser)
Igor Stravinsky, Symphony of Psalms (red.), pp. 31–32 (Boosey)

PERCUSSIVE USE OF HARMONY

Accents may be produced by any material that calls attention to itself through stress, duration, pitch level, tone quality, relative harmonic values, or repetition. The tonal equivalent of percussion rhythms (instruments of indeterminate pitch) is the melodic repeated note. Reiteration of the melodic tone is a rhythmic force that often stimulates repeated-chord activity. The rhythm of chordal repetition may act as a tonal stimulant in slow harmonic rhythm.

Ex. 10-15

Rhythm, both accentual and durational, can for a span of time serve as a chief compositional element. In answer to a drum figure, a chord may function percussively.

Ex. 10-16

An isolated chord may command attention when substituting for a bass drum stroke. If the chord is a sudden large compound chord or a low cluster, a harmonic sforzando may be produced. The introduction of a chord outside the key realm or a sudden increase in the number of parts may also produce a harmonic accent. Smaller intervals placed at the bottom of chords may produce harmonic percussiveness.

Ex. 10-17

Miscellaneous instruments sounding their lower notes accentuate the percussiveness of chords as the pitch projection is dampened.

Ex. 10-18

Source Material

Passages featuring repeated notes or chords:

Ernest Bloch, Piano Quintet, p. 72 (G. Schirmer)
Henry Cowell, Homage to Iran (violin and piano), p. 4 (Peters)
David Diamond, Rounds for String Orchestra, p. 1 (Elkan-Vogel)
Irving Fine, Partita for Wind Quintet, p. 32 (Boosey)
Bruno Maderna, Serenata No. 2 (for 11 instruments), pp. 25–30 (Zerboni)
Serge Prokofiev, Violin Concerto in D (red.), p. 21 (Breitkopf)
Carl Ruggles, Evocations for Piano, p. 3 (Am. Mus. Ed.)
Dmitri Shostakovich, Symphony No. 10, p. 151 (Leeds)
Roman Vlad, Sonatina for Flute and Piano, p. 18 (Zerboni)
Anton Webern, Symphonie Op. 21, p. 12 (Universal)

Passages featuring percussive harmony:

George Antheil, Five Songs 1919–1920, p. 8 (Cos Cob)
Béla Bartók, Piano Sonata, p. 13 (Universal)
Alban Berg, Wozzeck (red.), p. 215 (Universal)
Carlos Chávez, Sinfonia de Antigona, p. 4 (G. Schirmer)
Luigi Dallapiccola, Il Prigioniero (red.), p. 17 (Zerboni)
Manuel de Falla, Harpsichord Concerto, p. 4 (Eschig)
Arthur Honegger, Pacific 231, p. 4 (Senart)
Alan Hovhaness, Magnificat, p. 3 (Peters)
Jacques Ibert, Angélique (red.), p. 13 (Heugel)
Anton Webern, Six Pieces for Orchestra Op. 6, pp. 16–17 (Universal)

PANDIATONIC WRITING

A lack of harmonic rhythm (one chord) creates static harmony and a feeling of breadth or relaxation.

Ex. 10-19

Static harmony is useful when attention is to be focused upon a rhythmic motif, or when it is used in repeated chords, announcing the rhythm of an unaccompanied melody to follow.

Ex. 10-20

Pandiatonic writing is a specific kind of static harmony in which an entire scale is used to form the members of an implied secundal, static chord. The vertical structures are combinations of any number of tones from the prevailing scale, placed in variable spacings. The horizontal chord succession has no tonal direction; scale tones are manipulated as basic chordal material without creating harmonic motion outside the underlying static and unaltered scale. The harmony has no characteristic functions; the counterpoint is rhythmically active, and the chord spacing erratic. Melodic, contrapuntal, and vertical combinations may be underpinned by persistent intervals in the lower voices. Fifths and tenths from the bass are more fluent than thick thirds or stubborn fourths; fourths tend to predominate in the upper part of the chord, and seconds and sevenths harness the texture for early cadential arrivals. One mode is seldom used for an entire pandiatonic section, particularly a mode with no flats or sharps, for "white-key fever" is contracted easily.

In three-part harmony each succeeding chord often contains three fresh notes bringing all scale tones to aural consciousness in seven-tone static harmony. If ornamental tones are used in one chord, fresh notes are used as members of the following chord.

Ex. 10-21

Doubling is seldom employed, even in five- or six-part harmony.

Ex. 10-22

In seven-part harmony, the seven scale steps are constantly sounded.

Ex. 10-23

Any scale may be used as a basis for pandiatonicism. All the intervallic characteristics of any scale, synthetic or otherwise, can be projected pandiatonically at once.

Source Material

Static harmony:

Béla Bartók, Herzog Blaubarts Burg (red.), p. 51 (Universal)
Carlos Chávez, Sinfonia India, p. 63 (G. Schirmer)
Werner Egk, La Tentation de Saint Antoine, pp. 38–42 (Schott)
Colin McPhee, Four Iroquois Dances, pp. 3–9 (New Music)
Darius Milhaud, Cinq Symphonies (petit orchestre), pp. 2–4 (Universal)
Carl Orff, Die Sänger der Vorwelt (red.), pp. 3–16 (Schott)
Maurice Ravel, Concerto for Piano and Orchestra in G (red.), p. 26 (Durand)
Silvestre Revueltas, Cuauhnahuac, p. 14 (G. Schirmer)
Jean Sibelius, From the Land of Thousand Lakes, p. 9 (Boston)
Igor Stravinsky, Mass, pp. 6–7 (Boosey)

Pandiatonic writing:

William Bergsma, Tangents, Vol. II, p. 21 (C. Fischer)
Aaron Copland, Appalachian Spring, pp. 51–52 (Boosey)
Ingolf Dahl, Divertimento for Viola and Piano, p. 46 (G. Schirmer for S.P.A.M.)
Howard Hanson, The Lament of Beowulf (red.), pp. 16–19 (Birchard)
Arthur Honegger, Jeanne d'Arc au Bûcher (red.), p. 53 (Salabert)
Igor Stravinsky, Duo Concertant for Violin and Piano, p. 13 (Russe)

DYNAMICS AND RESTS

Dynamics are an essential element in composition. Harmonic progression is affected by the degree of dynamic nuance in which it is conceived. A dissonant and restless progression set in a pianissimo context is likely to explode into a subito forte of violent polychords, while the same progression in a forte context might find harmonic satisfaction in its overbearing tension and remain in the same harmonic sphere. Highly chromatic chords blend with more harmonic ease in soft passages than in loud.

Dynamics have a rhythm that is projected by means of piano, forte, crescendo, diminuendo, sforzando, and subito directions of accentuation. They reinforce the natural rhythm when they coincide with it, and create a contrary line of tension when they oppose it. If a crescendo is used through a passage of growing harmonic tension, overwhelming cumulative power may be obtained. If a diminuendo is used through the same kind of passage, quite a different kind of tension results. The rhythm of melody, harmony, and dynamic nuance generates musical forces that can be juxtaposed in many ways to create a variety of climactic conditions.

The rest is a potent creative factor. It may help lighten texture and project motivic figures.

Ex. 10-24

In multi-voice florid writing, voices rest periodically so that individual imitative parts are not obscured. Rests preceding fresh entrances add interest to long melodic lines. When transparency in texture is sought voices are widely spaced and rest often. Rests can increase harmonic momentum; an interruption of a high-tensioned chord by silence produces an undercurrent of harmonic expectation. In a whispering diminuendo temporary silences imply unwritten harmonic innuendos.

Rests have rhythmic power. In an established pattern of accents, a silent pulse has more strength than one sounded.

Ex. 10-25

A rest before a climactic chord adds power to the arrival.

Ex. 10-26

Source Material

Passages with characteristic dynamics and rests:

Franco Donatoni, Composizione in Quattro Movimenti (piano), p. 3 (Schott)

Bruno Maderna, Serenata No. 2 (for 11 instruments), p. 21 (Zerboni)
William Schuman, Judith, pp. 60–61 (G. Schirmer)
Igor Stravinsky, Symphonies of Wind Instruments (rev. 1947), p. 26 (Boosey)
Camillo Togni, Fantasia Concertante (flute and string orchestra), p. 32 (Zerboni)
Anton Webern, Variationen Op. 27, p. 6 (Universal)

Applications

1. Write a duettino for snare drum and tenor drum using asymmetric divisions of the measure.

2. Write a dance for piano in which change of meter is exploited.

3. In a three-part song form for clarinet, piano, and snare drum (snares off) manipulate the melodic rhythm of the clarinet, the harmonic rhythm of the piano, and the percussive rhythm of the snare drum so that each of the three formal sections contains a different set of rhythmic relationships.

4. Write a woodwind scherzo of erratic harmonic rhythm.

5. Write a fast passage for string quartet with slow harmonic rhythm.

6. Write a lyric piano prelude in which the harmonic accents frequently oppose the barline accents.

7. Write a Vivo for two pianos using simple chords that move so rapidly that they create a harmonically complex sound.

8. Syncopate the harmonic rhythm of four noisy stopped horns against a regular rhythm in low unison strings and brasses.

9. In a woodwind duo allow an oboe to play in triple time simultaneously with a bassoon playing in quadruple time. Adjust the tempo so that the bar lines coincide.

10. Write a string trio passage in which each instrument employs a different time signature with bar lines falling at different places.

11. Illustrate isorhythm in a flute, clarinet, and bassoon passage of quartal harmony.

12. Illustrate isomelos in a flute, oboe, clarinet, and bassoon passage of tertian harmony.

13. Employ melodic repeated notes and chordal repetition in a fiery passage for trumpet and string orchestra.

14. Pit the strength of percussive orchestral chords against a powerful, opposing timpani part.

15. Write a passage of percussive clusters in the lower regions of the orchestra.

16. Write a rough passage in the strings using percussive chords.

17. Exploit the principle of pandiatonicism in a short section for double string orchestra.

18. Write a gradual diminuendo for piano, four hands, in which the harmonic tension gradually increases.

19. Write a brass passage containing rests of great rhythmic power.

Embellishment and Transformation

ORNAMENTAL FIGURATION

VERTICAL STRUCTURES form a harmonic skeleton upon which melodic figuration may rest. These melodic embellishments may be harmonic or nonharmonic ornamental tones. The ornamental harmonic tones consist of repeated chord tones and broken-chord tones and create no intervallic resistance to the harmony. When ornamental figuration is created by chords that are broken in two or more voices, the individual parts gain freedom. Harmonic ornamentation may increase the space between chord changes and relax harmonic rhythm. Members of a broken chord sounded by a single voice may imply meaningful harmonic progression.

Ex. 11-1

Ornamental nonharmonic tones are inherently restless because of their intervallic counteraction to the chord. Nonharmonic tones may be either accented or unaccented; they are accented when they occur with the change of harmony, regardless of their place in the measure. There are four general kinds of nonharmonic tones: passing and auxiliary tones which are approached and left without skip;

Ex. 11-2

changing tones which are approached conjunctly and left by a skip (*a*); appoggiaturas which are approached by a skip and left conjunctly (*b*);

Ex. 11-3

and a hybrid group which includes those nonharmonic tones that are formed by the rhythmic misplacement of chord tones. In suspensions, the movement is delayed (*a*), and in anticipation the movement is hastened (*b*):

Ex. 11-4

It is possible to skip to and from a nonharmonic tone if that tone becomes a member of the following chord (*a*); while implying a larger formation over the same root (*b*); and while resisting any chordal affiliation (*c*).

Ex. 11-5

Before resolving, the nonharmonic tone itself may be ornamented by and combined with other ornamental tones.

Relatively simple harmony or held chords may be spiced by dissonant and free ornamentation.

Ex. 11-6

Ornamental tones may be derived from a scale built upon the root of the chord; each root is embellished as though it were a tonic.

Ex. 11-7

Ornamental patterns may be derived from contrasting key centers creating temporary polytonality.

Ex. 11-8

Nonharmonic tones may be grouped chord-wise and used as ornamental chords such as passing chords, auxiliary chords, and so on:

Ex. 11-9

The ornamental tone may remain unresolved, causing a change of harmonic texture.

Ex. 11-10

Simple chords may be embellished in such a way that one chord penetrates another, creating polychordal sounds where they meet.

Ex. 11-11

Source Material

Passages featuring ornamental figuration:

Luciano Berio, Cinque Variazioni per Pianoforte, p. 10 (Zerboni)
Werner Egk, Die Zaubergeige (red.), p. 173 (Schott)
Paul Hindemith, Sonata for Piano, Four Hands, pp. 30–31 (Schott)
Vincent Persichetti, Fourth Symphony, p. 107 (Elkan-Vogel)
Goffredo Petrassi, Invenzioni per Piano, pp. 20–21 (Zerboni)
Walter Piston, Trio for Violin, Cello and Piano, p. 1 (Arrow)
Serge Prokofiev, Piano Sonata No. 3, p. 5 (Leeds)
Arnold Schoenberg, Gurre-Lieder (red.), p. 165 (Universal)
Hugo Weisgall, Purgatory (red.), p. 4 (Merion)

EXTENSION AND IMITATION

The many motivic cells that make up a theme are the concern of the composer when extending harmonic material. The motivic fragments he chooses and the way in which he transforms them are elements that give a work its personal identity.

Repetition is one of the most important devices in musical composition. Repetition emerges as sequence, imitation, variation, ostinato, and in various other guises. Of the many techniques used by the composer to extend harmonic fabric, none is more trying than literal repetition. A strong sense of timing and a discriminating taste will determine when reiteration will not hinder musical flow.

Development of thematic material involves motivic metamorphosis; the life of a structural unit depends to a great extent upon the transformative character of its elements. Ascending sequence adds dynamic tension and descending sequential figures relax dynamic movement; sequences, whether melodic (tonal or real), harmonic, rhythmic, or in combination, soften extremely dissonant passages. In diminution, shortening of the rhythmic unit promotes drive; lengthening the time values (augmentation) lessens movement tension. Musical ideas may be extended in many ways. Characteristic elements may be intervallically expanded (a) or contracted (b),

Ex. 11-12

and the order changed.

Ex. 11-13

Whole passages or small segments may be inverted, revealing fresh melodic and harmonic aspects. Removing certain notes of the line creates hidden tone-relationships, and filling out of thematic material with ornaments produces additional segments for further extension. Part of an idea may be omitted by dismemberment and held for later expansion. Repeating tones and shifting their octave placement adds new color and meaning. Variants of the motif are made possible through retrogression, retrograde inversion, and rhythmic transformation, and although the original identity is often obscured, a unified musical expression may unfold.

Imitation is a form of repetition in which the motivic elements move from voice to voice. The imitation may be literal or it may occur in any of the forms of extension variation. Imitation is, by nature, a linear process and a valuable device in achieving meaningful part-writing and harmonic suppleness. The strictness of imitation is no measure of esthetic evaluation, nor is free imitation necessarily a sign of inventiveness. The success of the use of linear devices in a harmonic context depends largely upon the needs of the expressive climate in which they operate.

Source Material

Harmony containing extensive imitation:

Béla Bartók, String Quartet No. 5, p. 27 (Boosey)
Boris Blacher, Studie im Pianissimo (orchestra), p. 28 (Bote)
Roy Harris, Symphony No. 3, pp. 85–91 (G. Schirmer)
Paul Hindemith, Symphonie Mathis der Maler, pp. 16–20 (Schott)
Arnold Schoenberg, Verklärte Nacht (string orchestra), pp. 4–5 (Associated)
Anton Webern, Symphonie Op. 21, p. 8 (Universal)

CHROMATIC ALTERATION

The primary effect of chordal alteration is a change of harmonic color without a change of chordal function. Dissonance may be intensified (*a*) or lessened (*b*) by the alteration.

Ex. 11-14

An alteration does not exist as such unless a scale area is defined or unless a characteristic chord is used as a harmonic norm. In C major, the following example illustrates an altered first measure; but in C minor, the alteration is contained in the Picardian second measure.

Ex. 11-15

The altered formation must be foreign to the scale presently in effect. The chord G-Bb-Eb is an altered six-three (Neapolitan sixth) in D major, but in the D Double Harmonic scale it is the unaltered supertonic.

Ex. 11-16

Altered chords in the Oriental scale have "unaltered" major freshness.

Ex. 11-17

Chromatic lowering as an alteration causes a drop in textural tension, and chromatic raising gives a succession tonal lift. When altered chords are used in excess they lose touch with the unaltered harmonic norm and fail to function as altered structures.

Common alterations are those derived from the closest related keys. The major key based upon the cycle of fifths may borrow its accidentals from the major keys a fifth above and below the tonic, and from its relative minors and the tonic minor.

Ex. 11-18

accidentals from G, F, C mi. and rel. minors

Minor keys of this cycle may use accidentals from two tonal strands, those keys related to both the relative and parallel majors.

Ex. 11-19

accidentals from rel. keys of E♭ and C

In keys based upon a cycle of thirds, accidentals are derived from the keys that lie a major or minor third above or below the tonic.

Ex. 11-20

In synthetic scales, common alterations may be derived from areas reached by modulation. If chords from C Leading Whole-tone scale have modulated to chords of the Neapolitan Major scale, accidentals of D Neapolitan Major may occur in C Leading Whole-tone as common alterations:

Ex. 11-21

A cross relation exists when a tone in one voice of a chord is altered in another voice of the following chord. The tension created by this device is greater in simple harmony and barely felt in highly chromatic harmony. In harmony that uses all twelve tones with equal frequency, no such relationship is felt.

Cross relation occurs quite naturally in triads moving in chromatic third relationship.

Ex. 11-22

Cross relation between a chord tone and a nonharmonic tone is less noticeable.

Ex. 11-23

The simultaneous sounding of altered and unaltered tones has a pungent flavor. When it is created by ornamentation, the effect is fleeting. In major-minor compound harmony this sound is firmly fixed.

Source Material

Harmony with extensive alteration:

Alban Berg, Violin Concerto (red.), pp. 47–48 (Associated)
Ernest Bloch, Concerto Grosso No. 1, p. 5 (Birchard)
Arnold Schoenberg, Das Buch der Hängenden Gärten, p. 28 (Universal)
Roger Sessions, From My Diary, p. 6 (Marks)
Dmitri Shostakovich, Piano Quintet, p. 65 (Am-Rus)

PEDAL POINT AND OSTINATO

A pedal is a tone or tones sustained, repeated, or ornamented while other voices move through a succession of chords, some of which may be foreign to the pedal.

Ex. 11-24

If three or more tones are held, a pedal chord evolves.

Ex. 11-25

Polytonality is often suggested by triple pedal point.

Tonic pedals have repose and non-tonic pedals have restlessness. Final pedals are used to reinforce a tonality or allow time for a figuration to conclude its ornamental design. When pedals are placed a fifth or ninth below the main body of harmony, sheen and resonance are added.

An ostinato is a well-defined melodic segment insistently repeated. The tonal simplicity of ostinato helps clarify the texture of polytonal writing.

Ex. 11-26

The ostinato becomes melodically obstinate in an upper voice and obtrusive in a middle voice. When ostinatos occur simultaneously, harmonic tension rises.

Ex. 11-27

Source Material

Examples of pedals:

Lukas Foss, A Parable of Death (red.), p. 40 (C. Fischer)
Paul Hindemith, Sonata in C for Violin and Piano, p. 21 (Schott)
Arthur Honegger, Sonata No. 1 for Violin and Piano, p. 2 (Salabert)
Zoltán Kodály, Missa Brevis, p. 45 (Boosey)
Arnold Schoenberg, Suite für Klavier, Op. 25, pp. 10–12 (Universal)
William Schuman, New England Triptych, pp. 2–4 (Presser)
Igor Stravinsky, Perséphone (red.), pp. 43–45 (Russe)
William Walton, Viola Concerto (red.), p. 43 (Oxford)

Examples of ostinatos:

Samuel Barber, Excursions, p. 3 (G. Schirmer)
Norman Dello Joio, Meditations on Ecclesiastes, p. 20 (C. Fischer)
Carlisle Floyd, Susannah (red.), p. 44 (Boosey)
Wolfgang Fortner, Mouvements (piano and orchestra), p. 69 (Schott)
Paul Hindemith, Das Marienleben (1948), p. 57 (Schott)
Arthur Honegger, King David (red.), p. 9 (Foetisch)
Paul Nordoff, Lacrima Christi, pp. 2–4 (Mercury)
Robert Palmer, Toccata Ostinato for Piano (Elkan-Vogel)
Igor Stravinsky, Symphony of Psalms (red.), p. 3 (Boosey)
William Walton, Belshazzar's Feast (red.), p. 11 (Oxford)

UNISON WRITING

Unison writing implies the sounding of a line by various
media at the same pitch or at different octaves. Much use is made
of unison texture in twentieth-century composition; it has significant formal and coloristic functions. Its chief value in a harmonic scheme is its textural contrast. The success of unison writing
depends upon keen formal timing. Unison may be used for opening
or interrupting calls (*a*); fanfare flourishes (*b*);

Ex. 11-28

pastoral interludes (*a*); veiled lines placed octaves apart (*b*);

Ex. 11-29

antiphonal answers (*a*); added string power (*b*);

Ex. 11-30

or outlining harmonic activity with broken chords.

Ex. 11-31

Unison writing is effective when stating a theme without its harmonic fabric, contrasting a single line with a chordal mass, or adding strength to a loud, full passage. Unison is also used for subsiding sound, rushing octaves gathering power for a climax, to introduce a new tonal area by outlining the fresh scale, or to project rhythmic variants in a recitative style.

Source Material

Unison writing:

Conrad Beck, Aeneas Silvius-Symphonie, p. 28 (Schott)
Bruno Bettinelli, Fantasia for Piano, p. 4 (Ricordi)
Benjamin Britten, String Quartet No. 2, p. 44 (Boosey)
Charles Griffes, Piano Sonata, p. 15 (G. Schirmer)
Camargo Guarnieri, Piano Concerto No. 2 (red.), p. 3 (Associated)
Roy Harris, Piano Suite, p. 4 (Mills)
Marcel Mihalovici, Sinfonia Partita, p. 27 (Heugel)
Serge Prokofiev, Piano Sonata No. 7, p. 2 (Leeds)
Arnold Schoenberg, String Quartet No. 4, p. 63 (G. Schirmer)

Applications

1. Write a short piece for two flutes and two clarinets featuring nonharmonic tones.

2. Harmonize the following melody (for piano) so that each checked note becomes a nonharmonic tone.

Ex. 11-32

3. Write a woodwind passage featuring ornamental chords.

4. Write a melodic line for clarinet that stems from broken chords of various kinds.

5. Write several phrases for piano in which ornamental figuration is created by chord tones.

6. Write imitative music for two flutes at the interval of the tritone.

7. Write music for horn and tuba with imitation in augmentation.

8. Write a passage for two cellos that has imitation at a dissonant interval.

9. Create a pyramid in brasses by employing close imitative entrances.

10. Write a passage for string orchestra using several effective cross relations.

11. Write a short piece for organ featuring harmonic alteration.

12. Write an expressive harmonic progression for strings over or under a pedal tone in the French horn.

13. Extend the following passage for two oboes and two bassoons, featuring the double pedal.

Ex. 11-33

14. Write melodic fragments, appropriate for use as ostinatos.

15. Write a lively flute tune over a double-bass ostinato.

16. Write a string quartet passage in which two ostinatos are used simultaneously.

17. Write a unison theme for violas or cellos.

18. Increase the intensity of a harmonically strong orchestral passage by employing sudden unison writing.

| # Key Centers

TONALITY

THE TONAL MEANING of an isolated chord is indefinite; it may be a crucial or an ornamental chord of many keys, or it may belong to no key. When surrounded by other chords its meaning may be restricted to a single tonality, to two or more wavering tonalities; or if it has atonal intentions the fact can be made obvious. Tonality does not exist as an absolute. It is implied through harmonic articulation and through the tension and relaxation of chords around a tone or chord base. A particular style or period is not always limited to a predilection for a single kind of tonality. Twentieth-century music makes use of many degrees of tonality and employs many means for establishing them.

In a strong tonal context, all elements of progression are subordinate to the pull of the tonal center and a drive towards cadential realization. Traditional tonality depends upon scale and chord relationships for its organization. Usually three basic chords are needed to produce a feeling of tonality: one built upon a scale step above the tonic, one below the tonic, and the tonic itself. Harmony with tritone gravitation is helpful in establishing the center.

Tonality may be established by using tones of a scale as chordal roots in varying degrees of support of the central tonic: in balanced support by the subdominant and dominant to the tonic (*a*); in balanced support by the submediant and mediant (*b*);

Ex. 12-1

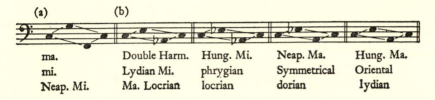

(a)	(b)			
ma.	Double Harm.	Hung. Mi.	Neap. Ma.	Hung. Ma.
mi.	Lydian Mi.	phrygian	Symmetrical	Oriental
Neap. Mi.	Ma. Locrian	locrian	dorian	lydian

in balanced support by the leading tone and supertonic (*a*); and in varying support by scale steps embracing the tritone (*b*).

Ex. 12-2

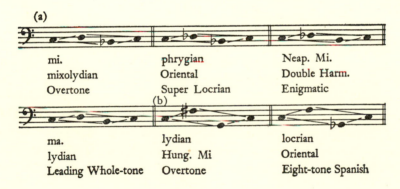

(a)		
mi.	phrygian	Neap. Mi.
mixolydian	Oriental	Double Harm.
Overtone	Super Locrian	Enigmatic

(b)		
ma.	lydian	locrian
lydian	Hung. Mi	Oriental
Leading Whole-tone	Overtone	Eight-tone Spanish

The remaining secondary scale roots decorate the three tonal pillars in each case.

Music may be brought into key focus by forces other than the tonal pull of chordal pillars. Key feeling may be created by an extremely dissonant chord refusing to become consonant, from a succession of simple chords resisting complex harmonic forces, from two culminating tonalities merging finally as a dominating polychord, from a group of important tones recurring at decisive points, or from atonal music searching for a key at cadential points.

Key consciousness may vanish temporarily only to make stronger an emerging key's return.

The search for tonality or key center feeling may become a creative force in music. The tonality of a structure may be generated from a unifying harmonic idea from which musical growth extends. An initial major-minor compound chord may promote polychordal writing that instigates a triadic struggle between major and minor structures; the formal conflict may not be resolved until an obstinate melody note, common to both triads, anchors them in a major-minor formation quite transposed from the original chord. A work may be built tonally upon an initial harmony that falls cadentially; the final cadence may find refuge in a group of tones far removed from the tonal implications of the first harmonic fall. A succession of chords at an opening may, in microcosm, suggest the tonal shape of the entire work. An insistent chord may establish a center by resisting pressures from various tonalities.

Ex. 12-3

Tonality may be established through contradictory tonal elements or through a streamlined drive to the tonic. In equidistant rootless harmony, any note may be made the tonal center through melodic insistence, spacing, or instrumentation.

Music may hold its tonality loosely, elements of atonality being inherent from the onset. There are many degrees of key-center gravity or of keylessness in the general area of tonality or atonality. At one extreme of the concept of key is tonality, the other extreme is atonality, and the point at which one ends and the other begins is indefinite. Melodic lines in a tonal framework can become so free that the implied harmony becomes evasively dissonant and a point reached where key feeling is lost. Partial atonality is useful in vague introductions and transition passages, and when preparing for a returning tonal thematic idea.

MODULATION

The ambiguity of any chord is such that it can be related to any of the twelve tonal centers. This is an important factor when modulating, a process of changing the tonal center. If a definite key change is desired, both keys should be firmly established by at least three center affirming chords. A pivotal chord is one that is common to both keys; it is diatonic when belonging to both scale formations and chromatic when it belongs to neither, or only to one. It is not always clear just which formation is the pivot chord —this only enhances modulatory beauty.

When modulating to a permanent key, chords other than the tonic may be aimed for so that time can be made for settling into the feeling of the new tonality. A premature cadence is avoided by jumping to a distant key, then working gradually toward the desired key.

Chromatic modulation is attained by shifting an entire chord a half step in sudden parallel harmony. Abrupt modulations make the arriving tonic felt as a distant chord; to establish a firm feeling of the new key, an extended harmonic progression is necessary in order to secure the new center. All chromatic tones are in the domain of a key when the vertical aspect gives way to the horizontal movement of voices; therefore, all keys have twelve tones in common and may be reached quickly chromatically.

Modulation may be realized through the semitone or other intervals. A fresh change is felt when the modulatory interval is one other than the characteristic interval of the prevailing root progression. Modulatory changes of the third relationship are effective in passages of second relationship harmony,

Ex. 12-4

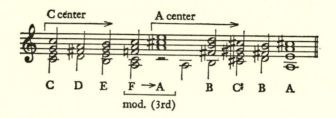

and changes of the second in third relationship harmony.

Ex. 12-5

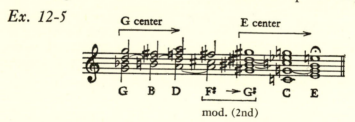

Key changes have special lift when modulation is accompanied by an octave leap in register.

Ex. 12-6

Continuous, quickly shifting keys produce a sense of displaced tonality rather than modulation.

Ex. 12-7

Key feeling may be gradually loosened or tightened. The gravity of a tonal center is decreased by moving a new voice through notes that give an important chord new roots.

Ex. 12-8

A distant tonality may be established by the reinforcement of the new center by auxiliary chords,

Ex. 12-9

or by the pneumatic action of violent repetitions of the new tonic with color and spacing changes.

Transient modulation is an important means of securing variety in relatively consonant passages. It is less effective in very dissonant passages. Chromatically complex harmony does not need the color of transitory modulation. In this harmonic context, modulation is used to move from one section to another, rather than within a progression itself.

Modulation from a single tonality to a polytonality may be attained by moving double strands of transient modulation in a contrary motion of keys. A coupled tonic makes an excellent starting point.

Ex. 12-10

When modulating from one polytonal area to another, each key zone usually moves to the new zone by independent modulatory means; the over-all harmonic total must, however, have textural design and intelligible tension fluctuation.

Distant tonal centers are reached in countless ways, but unless

this facile technique is held in careful check, harmonic growth will
be replaced by superficial variety.

POLYTONALITY

Polytonal writing is a procedure in which two or more keys are
combined simultaneously. If only two keys are sounded, the
specific term bitonality may be used, but polytonality has come
generally to imply the use of more than one tonal plane at the
same time. The scales that form the different tonic centers may be
intervallically identical or contrasting, traditional or synthetic.

Ex. 12-11

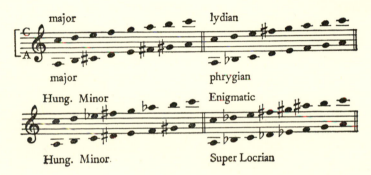

Great concern must be given the vertical factor; if tonal planes
are arbitrarily combined the harmonic result will be haphazard.
The music must be conceived in polytonal context, not cloaked in
accidental texture. Each melodic line should retain its own individuality yet the harmonic total must have direction of flow,
tension design, and textural consistency. Although each tonal
plane has its own organizational center, a single over-all tonic
structure is usually felt from the bass. From this basic polychordal
tonic stems the polytonal texture.

The following example employs C, E, and G areas at different
levels, but they combine in a total harmonic sound with C function-
ing as the fundamental:

Ex. 12-12

Polytonality, then, is a specific kind of tonal organization, a means of moving groups of voices within confined harmonic register areas. Polychordal writing is often tonal, and when each group of voices within a chordal unit functions within the confines of a stable scale zone, polytonality occurs.

Polytonality is effective as such only when each tonal plane is kept within a clear scale formation. Shifting of modality through chromatic alteration clouds the texture or simply produces miscellaneous polychords. For maximum clarity in the projection of different tonalities, one key is introduced and as the next key is added, the preceding key, having been established, becomes less obvious.

Ex. 12-13

The scale steps spanning the tritone should be brought into play as soon as possible; otherwise polytonality will fail to operate. In the following example, the lower F major strand has no B♭ or E, and the upper C major strand has no F or B; the result is ambiguously major.

Ex. 12-14

Closely spaced polytonal areas become muddy. The keys should be kept far enough apart to allow room for voice activity. Harmonic parts of three keys placed a small interval apart run into each other. Cramped polytonality of this type is possible but lacks versatility.

Independent lines should not be placed at random without an understanding of polytonal construction. The fundamental quality of polytonal texture is determined by the key relationship set up by the tonics. In major-key combinations, a polytonal order of tension from consonant to dissonant is secured by combining two keys that lie a perfect fifth, major ninth, major sixth, major third, major seventh apart—and so on up the cycle of fifths. The high point of resonance in the order is at the center.

Ex. 12-15

Those keys that are not closely related according to the circle of fifths will more easily set apart the tonal key spheres. The tritone as a basis for key coalition forms a prime polytonal relationship because it is the most resonant of the dissonant combinations of keys. Polytonal combinations of major keys are:

Ex. 12-16

Similar inventory should be made of all key combinations. When minor keys are at the bottom (major or minor at the top), fewer consonant combinations of keys are possible because of the minor third in the lower key.

When combining more than two keys, the consonant-dissonant order of resonance is: all keys separated by a perfect fifth, a major ninth, a major sixth, a major third, etc.

Ex. 12-17

When the intervals between the keys are not the same, the larger interval is found between the bottom keys. When combining three or more mixed keys, the uppermost key is governed by the resonant relationship to the bottom, not inner key.

The resonance of polytonality depends upon the resonance of the over-all tonic formation as determined by its intervallic tension. The passing secondary textures are maneuvered around the most resonant polychords that form the structural pillars of the particular key combination.

Ex. 12-18

These secondary textures often become thick and troublesome and are made workable by omission of chord members, doubling of stronger intervals, ornamental coloring, unison and two-part interpolations, or by ostinatos.

Polytonality may be established by two or more tonal planes of harmonic writing (chordal polytonality),

Ex. 12-19

or through imitative writing (horizontal polytonality). Real canons at intervals other than the octave can imply polytonality. Two or three lines may produce transparent polytonality.

Ex. 12-20

Block chords against a single contrasting key line create supple polytonal patterns; shifting pedals ease the polytonal texture.

Ex. 12-21

Well-balanced polytonality is secured through mirror scales (polymodality).

Ex. 12-22

ATONALITY

Atonality is a term loosely applied to music in which a definite key feeling has been weakened or lost, and to music in which no key gravitation ever existed. Atonal writing is the organization of sound without key establishment by chordal root relationships; but tone combinations or areas may form an atonal equivalent of tonality. In atonal music, relations between tones occur without reference to a diatonic scale formation. There is movement to and from characteristic intervallic formations but the central force is usually melody, and not a governing harmonic base. Atonality operates within a syntax that favors dissonant formations, and its organization is based upon shifting intervallic tension or an order of tones.

Atonal movement is often linear but may produce vertical combinations of mixed intervals (compound harmony) that are free from the power of an overbearing tonic. When the motion of voices causes a constant and total dissonance, beds of sound are created upon which prominent melodic lines may lie. If chromatic chordal mixtures accumulate, formal coherence is achieved by repetition, variation, or mutation of the chromatic sound groups. Although the harmonic factors are dependent upon melodic relationships, these vertical structures are often manipulated as a contributing element in atonal composition.

The various elements in atonal music are tightly knit by extreme motivic concentration, and reference is constantly made to previous material. There is little regular rhythmic stamping and no continuous chain rhythms; the rhythmic patterns are asymmetrical and the meters irregular and often complicated.

When the controlling principle of scalar tonality is abandoned, chordal root organization of the twelve tones ceases to exist, and form and unity are created by melodic and rhythmic development. A basic order of tones, all twelve or fewer, may be used as a unifying basis for a work, and formal devices evolve from the basic shape. Twelve-tone technique or composition with "twelve notes related to one another" is primarily a contrapuntal practice. It is essentially a polyphonic conception with some points in common with the pre-"tonal" music of the Middle Ages. Twelve-tone writing is, therefore, most naturally approached in a treatise on counterpoint.

SERIAL HARMONY

Harmony, even when secondary, is an important consideration in linear music. When harmony is regulated by a horizontal, unifying idea (twelve-tone or not), the texture may be serial; this kind of writing creates harmony of extraordinary compactness through the manifold variations of the motif relationships. Chordal formations that arise from serial linear writing have little or no function in a scalar tonal sense. Harmonic obligations arise from a chromaticism set up in harmonic areas from a characteristic series or portion of a series of tones. Logical melodic thinking gives the individual parts their direction and the ear of the composer gives them the quality of chordal movement.

Some directions in serial composition point away from the specialized craft of strict "atonal" writing, where all elements are generated from a single germ cell, toward a flexible creative process that includes the vast musical resources of composition, both tonal and atonal. The techniques and materials of atonal music are often amalgamated with those of many types of tonal idioms; the harmonic stock includes endless possible harmonic combinations. A synthesis of harmonic potentialities includes chord materials governed by root progressions, intervallic texture tensions, and serial

devices. At any point in the formal shape a melodic group of notes
may control harmonic texture. Any succession of any number of
tones, not necessarily all different (*a*), may be used in two or
more voices at once, forming harmony from horizontal movement
(*b*) or divided between voices, forming harmony from vertical
telescoping (*c*).

Ex. 12-23

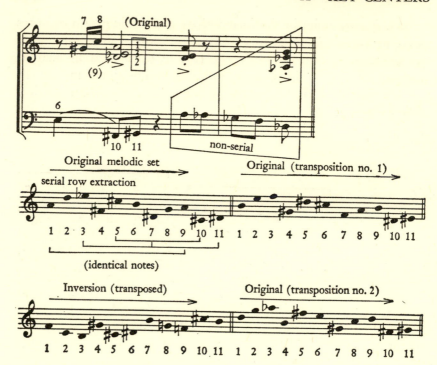

In an extended passage or section of free serial music, any combination of tones may be set up as a tonality. A succession of three or more notes from the selected melodic set or row of tones may be used as a center chord (*a*). A transposition of the center chord erected upon its uppermost note may form a cadential chord above the center (*b*); a mirror of the center chord may form another primary chord below (*c*). Changing the octave pitch of one or more tones produces inversions. Inversion of the center chord may yield a new set of primary chords (*d*, *e*, and *f*). All other combinations of tones may form secondary harmony.

Ex. 12-24

When a melodic set includes one or more identical notes, doubling of chord members produces colorful serial doublings. Parallel harmony may be used momentarily at points where doubling occurs.

Ex. 12-25

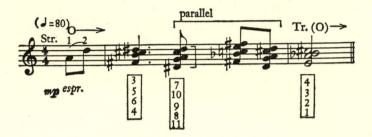

In serial harmonic progression, the order of chords is often changed to increase the gravitational tendency of the chordal formations to move to the center chord.

Ex. 12-26

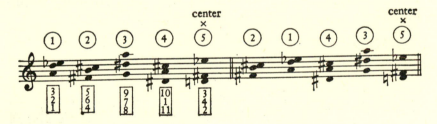

Transposition of the melodic set causes modulatory shifting of the harmonic areas.

Ex. 12-27

When a chord from one form (original, retrograde, inversion, or retrograde inversion in any transposition) of the melodic set is identical to a chord of another form of the set, it may be used as a pivot formation when entering new "tonal" areas. Closely related harmonic areas are those that may be found by constructing an inversion or retrograde inversion of the melodic set starting a perfect fifth above or below the original set.

Strong cadences may be formed by the primary chords (Ex. 12-24) or by ornamental movement of the parts directed toward the center chord.

Ex. 12-28

Chords may be ornamented by nonharmonic tones (*a*), by harmonic tones (*b*), or by serial tones that result from the simultaneous use of two or more forms of the set (*c*).

Ex. 12-29

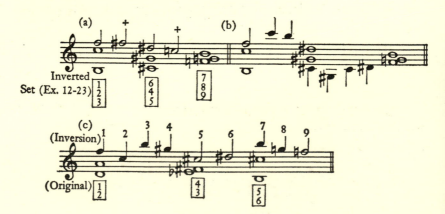

Contrasting thematic material may be built upon a new but related melodic set. The original set may be converted to another by selecting the top notes of a series of telescoped chords.

Ex. 12-30

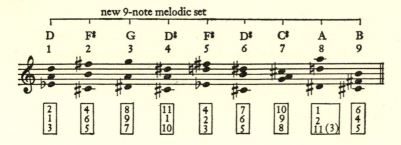

When melodic sets employ twelve different notes, successive chords encompass the entire twelve-tone field. A strong center or harmonic area may result from the completion or fulfillment of the twelve-tone set. Serial music of any type of row or set construction must be aurally created by melodic, harmonic, contrapuntal, rhythmic, and formal elements of the musical structure and not alone by manipulative procedures. Serial technique does not in itself insure communication or even effective sound organization any more than any other technique does. When automatic writing is avoided, the unifying power of serial practice allows great harmonic variety.

Source Material

Modulatory passages:

Ernest Bloch, Piano Quintet, pp. 57–59 (G. Schirmer)
Aaron Copland, The Tender Land (red.), pp. 67–68 (Boosey)
Ingolf Dahl, Sonata Seria for Piano, p. 14 (Presser)
Jacques Ibert, Histoires for Piano, p. 3 (Leduc)
Gian Carlo Menotti, The Unicorn, the Gorgon and the Manticore (red.),
    p. 56 (Ricordi)

Vincent Persichetti, Hymns and Responses for the Church Year, p. 1
   (Elkan-Vogel)
Serge Prokofiev, Second Violin Concerto (red.), p. 21 (Russe)
Arnold Schoenberg, Gurre-Lieder (red.), p. 146 (Universal)
Harold Shapero, Sonata for Violin and Piano, p. 13 (Southern)
Igor Stravinsky, Symphony in Three Movements, p. 78 (Associated)

Tonality created by non-traditional means:

Peter Racine Fricker, Concerto for Piano and Orchestra (Schott)
Hans Werner Henze, Concerto for Piano and Orchestra (Schott)
Paul Hindemith, Sonata in C for Violin and Piano (Schott)
Arthur Honegger, Violin Sonata No. 1 (Salabert)
Franco Margola, Piano Sonata 1956 (Ricordi)
Francis Poulenc, Mass in G major (Rouart-Lerolle)
Harold Shapero, Three Piano Sonatas (G. Schirmer)
Igor Stravinsky, Symphonie en Ut (Schott)

Examples of polytonality:

Benjamin Britten, The Turn of the Screw (red.), p. 158 (Boosey)
Alfredo Casella, 11 Pezzi Infantili, p. 20 (Universal)
Manuel de Falla, Harpsichord Concerto, p. 3 (Eschig)
Rodolfo Halffter, Piano Sonata No. 2, p. 31 (Peer)
Paul Hindemith, String Quartet No. 3, p. 21 (Schott)
Arthur Honegger, Symphony for Strings, pp. 28–30 (Salabert)
Darius Milhaud, Cinq Symphonies (petit orchestre) p. 61 (Universal)
Wallingford Riegger, New and Old (piano), p. 31 (Boosey)
Igor Stravinsky, Symphonies of Wind Instruments (red.), p. 14 (Russe)
Karol Szymanowski, String Quartet Op. 37, p. 19 (Universal)

Works with prominent atonality:

Alban Berg, Wozzeck (Universal)
Arthur Honegger, Pacific 231 (Senart)
Charles Ives, Aeschylus and Sophocles (from 19 Songs), (New Music)
Carl Ruggles, Evocations for Piano (Am. Mus. Ed.)
Arnold Schoenberg, Pierrot Lunaire (Universal)

Works written in free serial technique:

Aaron Copland, Piano Fantasy (Boosey)
Luigi Dallapiccola, Il Prigioniero (Zerboni)
Irving Fine, String Quartet No. 1 (C. Fischer)
Wallingford Riegger, Symphony No. 3 (Associated)
George Rochberg, String Quartet No. 1 (C. Fischer)
Roger Sessions, Symphony No. 2 (G. Schirmer)
Igor Stravinsky, Agon (Boosey)
Fartein Valen, Sonetto di Michelangelo (Norsk)

Applications

1. Write a woodwind passage whose basic tonality is E♭ with a strong tritone emphasis on A major.

2. Harmonize the following melody for string quartet, preserving the E tonal center.

Ex. 12-31

3. Write a passage for piano, four hands, in which an insistent chord establishes a center by resisting tonal pressures from various keys.

4. Compose a short dance for clarinet and piano which employs shifting tonality.

5. Write two-part counterpoint for the harpsichord with each part in a different tonality.

6. Extend the following polytonal passage for harpsichord (C mixolydian and E♭ aeolian):

Ex. 12-32

7. Extend the following polytonal passage for string trio (F♯ major and F lydian):

Ex. 12-33

8. Extend the following polytonal passage for piano (D♭ and C major):

Ex. 12-34

9. Write a short piano piece as follows:

A–two distant keys   RH–single line
                        LH–broken chords

B–two close keys   RH–chords
                    LH–ostinato

A–modified repetition with coda.

10. Write an orchestral example of polytonality with agile ninth chords in the woodwinds, sustained triads in the horns, and an ostinato (in tenths) in the low strings and winds.

11. Write a non-serial string-quartet example of atonal music.

12. Write a short piece for woodwind quintet that contains both serial and non-serial music.

| # Harmonic Synthesis

COMBINING TEXTURES

CONTEMPORARY harmonic writing is often a composite process
which may involve varying placement of the norm of dissonance,
choice of a single harmonic idiom or the coalition of one with another, fusion of tonalities, singleness of sound organization or the
juxtaposition of tonal and atonal aspects. The amalgamation of
divergent conceptions of tonal formations is part of our harmonic
language. Acceptance of one procedure does not necessarily mean
the exclusion of others. A fugue may be written over a cantus
firmus, a hymn placed under a tone row, and quartal harmony
blended with tertian.

The vertical combination of harmonic textures produces polychordal and compound formations, but successive combinations
entail movement from one kind of texture to another and the func-
tioning of heterogeneous harmonic materials side by side. A textural problem arises from the manipulation of the transitional materials that lead from one type of harmony to another. The characteristic interval of one kind of harmony is contained in any other

kind of harmony and may be brought to the surface by intervallic inversion. In all textural changes, an interval may be featured that, when inverted, produces the characteristic interval of the new harmony. The interval of the fourth is given a prominent position in chords by thirds to allow chords by fourths to enter; the fifth contained in the triad is inverted to allow for oncoming fourths (*a*). In seventh chords the inverted fifth from the root or third may be used to introduce quartal harmony (*b*). The voices of an inverted seventh chord may be arranged so that the interval of the second is emphasized and the contextual way prepared for secundal harmony (*c*). In ninth chords the interval of the seventh from the root or third is inverted to suggest the secundal texture of clusters or added-note chords (*d*).

Ex. 13-1

When moving from one type of harmony to another the characteristic interval of the new harmony is best introduced well in advance. The doubling of a colorful tone (major third, major seventh, or prominent nonharmonic tone) strongly suggests octave or unison writing that in turn makes way for foreign harmonic resources. The unison can become a supple device for moving from one kind of texture to another. The harmonic ambiguity or sudden unison allows for the entrance of any texture. The versatile ornamental tone also provides textural means for entering any harmonic region. The appoggiatura and suspension are particularly effective in preparing the intervallic texture. The melodic freedom of broken chords permits the fluctuation of chords of varying construction.

Ex. 13-2

Accenting melodic tones that outline the characteristic intervallic formation of the new area creates a tonal bond between the contrasting harmonic materials.

Ex. 13-3

The type of chordal formation may be changed by subtracting from a melodic motif tones that leave only the tones of the new texture.

Ex. 13-4

The equidistant chord has neither root nor power to resist homogeneous chordal formations and can, by chromatic motion, weave one harmonic fabric into another. Rough tritone relationship or prominent hidden fifths divert attention from harmonic transformations. Sequential patterns can drive varied chords over many harmonic barriers.

A common transitional harmonic device involving clusters is the gradual subtraction of cluster members, leaving chords that suggest the kind of harmony to follow. The reverse is no less effective.

Ex. 13-5

Polychords are approached through coupled triads (*a*), or chromatic conversion of chords (*b*). Motion from polychords to triads is created by the evaporation of one triad of the poly-chord (*c*).

Ex. 13-6

The harmonic units of a tonal polychordal succession may meet at a point where each progresses in a separate and consistent key zone. The polychordal progression then becomes polytonal. Aton-ality may be entered through florid writing when the individual lines are given such freedom of chromatic movement that the im-plied harmony becomes indefinite and the feeling of key disappears.

THEME AND FORM IDEAS

A melodic kernel of two or more tones may form the nucleus from which the subject matter of an entire work is shaped and har-mony derived. The compositional process is meaningless unless thematic statements are identifiable, for continuity and coherence are effected through aural retention of motifs. It is imperative that a sense of tempo, dynamics, and medium be part of thematic conception. Even a single tone can serve as a point of departure through dynamic and timbre implications; a pianissimo and expressive middle C played by a solo viola has musical impetus while a rough, staccato, and loud middle C played by three trombones has a quite different kind of musical energy.

Creative momentum might stem from a scale formation, a series of non-scale tones, a chordal structure, a lone tone repeating itself before finding a new tone from which flight can be made, the melodic contour formed by a complex opening chord attempting to shed its dissonant tones, or themes shaped by brasses answering a loud timpani. Material might be born of creative tension caused by pattern shapes: the excitement of fast-moving voices of sopranos, the intrigue of brass figures accompanying a resounding string section, or the richness of strings under a unison melody in the solo piano.

Careful inventory of melodic, rhythmic, and harmonic aspects of thematic ideas must be taken, because as a work progresses these elements are often used independently of each other. Not until full thematic intelligibility is realized do hidden meanings of the theme come to the surface. Thematic ideas may be purposefully enigmatic and vague, positive and complete in themselves, or musically neutral, but they should be positively vague, not vaguely positive. The composer must be fully aware of the potentialities of his material so that full advantage can be taken of the phenomenon of thematic transformation. Thematic meaningfulness can arise only from thematic unity and purpose. If a theme is not nourished by its motivic constituents it will lack significance.

Form and style are inseparably related. Form is the outward equivalent of instinct, taste, and style, and is the manner in which kinds of materials are presented. Divergent musical materials may be brought out of context into a piece, but the success of the decision to change the prevailing milieu depends upon creative sensitivity. Conflicting formal elements often result in free and imaginative forms, and the whole course of a major work is altered. The impulse that incites the composer to deviate from the predictable must at the same time create a feeling of inevitability of form.

Association of musical ideas is created by the melodic motif, the harmonic succession, and the rhythmic pattern; none of these three formal elements becomes functional until it is transformed by the creative musical process. It is during this growth that specific ideas for shaping the formal structure stimulate creative writing: a succession of simple chords fighting dissonant forces may succeed or fail; an extremely dissonant and overbearing chord refusing to become consonant may produce a distinctive harmonic progression; a succession of chords, dramatically placed, may indicate the formal direction; a work may be built upon initial harmony falling cadentially; provocative formal elements may be introduced by brightening the harmony as notes get slower and darkening the harmony as notes get faster; six taped microtones may be electronically upset by hexachordal diapasons that push agitated *Sprechstimme* fragments against tuned oriental blocks.

Any tone can succeed any other tone, any tone can sound simultaneously with any other tone or tones, and any group of tones can be followed by any other group of tones, just as any degree of tension or nuance can occur in any medium under any kind of stress or duration. Successful projection will depend upon the contextual and formal conditions that prevail, and upon the skill and soul of the composer.

Source Material

Passages containing various kinds of harmonic textures:

Alban Berg, Violin Concerto (red.), pp. 47–48 (Universal)
Paul Hindemith, Six Chansons (II), (Associated)
Arthur Honegger, Piano Concertino, pp. 1–4 (Senart)
Charles Ives, Violin Sonata No. 4, p. 8 (Arrow)
Michael Tippett, String Quartet No. 3, p. 1 (Schott)

Works containing contrasting techniques:

Béla Bartók, Piano Concerto No. 2 (Boosey)
Karl Amadeus Hartmann, Symphony No. 6 (Schott)
Charles Ives, Piano Sonata No. 2 (Concord), (Arrow)
Vincent Persichetti, Quintet for Piano and Strings (Elkan-Vogel)
Roman Vlad, Divertimento for 11 Instruments (Boosey)

Unique thematic ideas:

Béla Bartók, String Quartet No. 4, p. 3 (Boosey)
Alban Berg, Violin Concerto, p. 1 (Universal)
John Cage, Amores for Prepared Piano, p. 1 (New Music)
Carlos Chávez, Sinfonia India, p. 1 (G. Schirmer)
Aaron Copland, Vitebsk (violin, cello and piano), p. 1 (Cos Cob)
Roy Harris, Concerto for Piano, Clarinet and String Quartet, p. 39 (Cos Cob)
Luigi Nono, Coro di Didone, p. 1 (Scherchen)
Wallingford Riegger, Dichotomy, p. 1 (New Music)
Guido Turchi, Preludi e Fughetti per Pianoforte, p. 4 (Zerboni)
Roman Vlad, Sonatina for Flute and Piano, p. 2 (Zerboni)
Ralph Vaughan Williams, Symphony No. 6, p. 143 (Oxford)

Works with unique forms:

Béla Bartók, Music for String Instruments, Percussion and Celesta (III), (Boosey)
Alban Berg, Lyric Suite (III), (Universal)
Luciano Berio, Cinque Variazioni per Pianoforte (Zerboni)
Pierre Boulez, Improvisation sur Mallarmé (Universal)
Sylvano Bussotti, Five Piano Pieces for David Tudor (Universal)
Elliott Carter, String Quartet No. 2 (Associated)
Carlos Chávez, Sonatina for Violin and Piano (New Music)
Alois Hába, Suite No. 3 for Quarter-Tone Piano (Universal)
Roy Harris, Symphony No. 3 (G. Schirmer)
Paul Hindemith, Hin und Zurück (Schott)
Charles Ives, The Unanswered Question (Southern)
Bo Nilsson, Zwanzig Gruppen (Universal)
Vincent Persichetti, Harmonium (soprano and piano), (Elkan-Vogel)
Gunther Schuller, String Quartet No. 1 (III), (Universal)
William Schuman, Symphony No. 6 (G. Schirmer)
Karlheinz Stockhausen, Klavierstücke I–IV (Universal)
Igor Stravinsky, Symphonies of Wind Instruments (Russe)
Edgard Varèse, Ionisation (New Music)
Anton Webern, Five Pieces for String Quartet Op. 5 (Universal)

Applications

1. Write a passage in any medium containing the following chords (among others) in any order and in any transposition.

Ex. 13-7

2. Extend the following idea in the string orchestra and include various categories of harmony.

Ex. 13-8

3. Weave a passage of organ music through tertian, quartal, secundal, polychordal, and compound harmony.

4. Construct thematic material on the following pattern ideas: rich string harmony under a solo trumpet; fast-moving woodwinds; huge declamatory chords for two pianos; solo timpani answered by full orchestra; string and woodwind chords surrounded by virtuoso figures in the brasses; coupled two-part writing in the band; percussive harpsichord chords with abbreviated ornaments; lyric polytonality in the oboe and guitar; dynamic chords in the harp with frequent two-part interruptions in the flute and viola; a soprano vocalise with mirror writing in the piano; clustered brasses with melodic writing in the timpani and xylophone; quiet ornamented polychords in the organ; quartal harmony in the woodwind quintet with erratic harmonic rhythm; vivacious pandiatonic writing in the mixed chorus on a phrase from one of the Psalms; and a virtuoso keyboard mirror for solo piano.

5. Make piano reductions of provocative passages from several twentieth-century orchestral works.

Index of Composers

Subject Index